STATE RAISED

STATE RAISED

A Deep Look into the World of Prison

MATT WRIGHT

iUniverse, Inc.
New York   Bloomington

State Raised
A Deep Look into the World of Prison

iUniverse books may be ordered through booksellers or by contacting:

iUniverse
1663 Liberty Drive
Bloomington, IN 47403
www.iuniverse.com
1-800-Authors (1-800-288-4677)

Because of the dynamic nature of the Internet, any Web addresses or links contained in this book may have changed since publication and may no longer be valid.

The views expressed in this work are solely those of the author and do not necessarily reflect the views of the publisher, and the publisher hereby disclaims any responsibility for them.

ISBN: 978-0-595-43621-7 (pbk)
ISBN: 978-0-595-87945-8 (ebk)

Printed in the United States of America

Contents

Jason Suydam: Twenty-two years old and incarcerated for a sex offense, a gay man comes to terms with his sexuality while evolving into adulthood in the cruelest of all worlds.

Samuel "C-Mike" Turner: A gang member's story of transition, describing how the negative elements of prison culture and lifestyle helped to mold him into a positive member of society.

Bill Van Court: A lifelong substance abuser who was in and out of jails and prisons for drug-seeking charges until age thirty-two, when the State of Washington labeled him a habitual offender and sentenced him to spend the rest of his life in prison.

Laurence Johnson: As Laurence went from better to bitter, the race to the top put him on the bottom. How having a blue-collar life with all the promise of comfort became a life of black and white stripes living in a six-by-nine closet with a toilet.

Johnni H.: A former married University of Washington football player who led a secret life of homosexual affairs and drug abuse that all came crum-

bling apart when he was convicted of drug charges, sentenced to four years in prison, and then became HIV positive while incarcerated.

Katie Wright: *After the death of my little sister, Katie, my big sister, Theodora, mailed me this story she wrote. Hearing my sister's fear, pain, and distress over my situation has guided and hurt me every day since. Until I read her story, I never knew how much someone could love me and how much I could hurt the ones I love.*

The Goad

Personal Property Matrix

Visiting Room Guidelines

Minor Infraction Codes

Classification Reports

Major Infraction Codes

Preface: Prison Reality

Prison is full of desperate people who will do anything to satisfy their desires. Money, drugs, or status within the prison gives you a kind of power that you can use to get others to do your bidding. Many people don't have anything, so the prisoners that do are in a position to get what they need or want.

Prisoners with power can have the best of everything—pillows, mattresses, cells, tables, homosexuals, food, jobs, drugs, clothes, mission boys, associates—anything you can think of, power can get you. People will do anything to please and impress you.

I know people with power who have had other prisoners beaten up, sexually assaulted, stabbed, held down to have tattoos covered up or cut out of their skin, vandalized (their personal property), intimidated, or sabotaged when it came to jobs, cells, tables, or status. This may be because they do not like the way someone laughs, farts, or smells; because they are dirty or have a charge they don't like. They might want to remove someone from population and have him sent to protective custody (or transferred) so they can take over his drug business, set an example, or settle a score for themselves or others.

In prison, if you use your power the right way you can position yourself so that even if people hate you they can't do anything about it. My code of survival: information is knowledge, knowledge is power, power is control, control is happiness, happiness is peace, and peace helps me sleep.

You don't have to be a shot caller or in a gang to be in charge of the situation around you. But as with everything else, having power and having people know that you have power can be a harsh curse. No amount of power can get people to like you if you're not likable or to forget a charge that is despicable. As fast as the people around you become loyal to you, they can turn on you. The population can become jealous easily, and they love to tear people apart—all they need is a reason. The predators are always circling and looking for ways to get ahead.

There are some hardcore individuals in prison. They know what they want and will do whatever it takes to get it. This life becomes their life, and they will live it until they die. I watched as a shot caller placed a razor blade on a dayroom table and forced another prisoner to cut out a tattoo that he thought the guy did not deserve to wear. I know another prisoner that had a guy killed over a five-dollar joint. I know a few prisoners that have started riots just to see who was down to riot with them and who wasn't.

Most of the violence happens behind closed doors in prison, and whatever takes place or what you see is none of your business. I got into a fight with a guy once in a cell. I was very bruised up and he had a bad cut over his eye. I couldn't go to medical for help, because if I did, they would ask what happened and when I said I can't remember they would place me in the hole on administrative segregation (Ad-Seg) and then the guards would go cell to cell to check fists and faces for any marks or bruises.

This is my problem; it is my responsibility not to allow my problems to affect the prisoners around me, whether I know them or not. They are doing whatever they are doing, and if I bring attention to them I could be creating problems for myself in the future.

All I can do is go back to my cell and stay until the bruising goes away. I can't go to the chow hall, phones, visit room, dayroom, or anywhere. If I don't have store in the cell, I have to rely on others to lend me store or smuggle food back from the chow hall for me. I didn't leave the cell for ten days, but I was lucky, because the guy I was fighting had a cut above his eye and he had to use a needle and thread to stitch himself up and did not leave his cell for a few weeks.

Sexual assaults, pressuring, and predatory behavior is common. When you step off the chain bus, the population is watching and waiting. On chain days, some prisoners get all dressed up in their best clothes and wait in the chow hall to see the new faces, and if they're interested, they invite them over to impress them, buy them, or pressure them.

They send other prisoners to test you and see how you will respond or have them threaten and pressure you so they can come running to you to be a hero and tell you how they will protect you. There is no difference between a drug addict looking for a fix and any kind of predator searching for prey. They all get this glossed-over look in their eyes, and all you can do is your own thing.

So many mind games and tricks are pulled on the weaker prisoners that they are always in a tough spot. If they tell, they are placed in segregation for their own protection and months later transferred, and then the prisoners at their new prisons label them snitches and attack and torment them and their cycle starts all over.

Their only real choices are to accept what is happening to them or fight. If they do fight, the prison system then labels them a management problem. This ensures they go to or remain in the harder prisons, where other prisoners are waiting, and they'll continue to be tested or taken advantage of. The saying is "fuck or fight," and if you don't start out fighting, prisoners will always be waiting to take their shots.

I've seen guys fall in love with other guys and become so obsessed or possessive that they stab others, beat others up, or get beaten themselves. One guy got so upset when he could not stop his homosexual mate from being transferred that he wrapped toilet paper all over his naked body, poured gas on himself, and set himself on fire.

Once, a very feminine white homosexual who was with some white guys was seen talking with a known black homosexual. Two white guys went into his cell and beat him down, then put both of his legs on the stool and stomped on them until they broke. The screaming coming from the cell was nightmarish.

When a drug addict gets strung out or cut off from his dope, he will do anything he can dream of for a fix—beg and cry to their families, have people call their families and tell them that they will be killed if they don't send money somewhere, sell themselves and any possessions they have, become a mission boy or mule. Some will fake injuries for prescription pills, while others will inflict real injury on themselves, throwing themselves down stairs or slamming their hands in doors. I know a guy who faked passing kidney stones by cutting the tip of his dick to pee blood into a cup.

The spread of disease is a big problem. Most homosexuals go from guy to guy regularly. Needles are expensive and hard to hide, so most are just passed around from dope fiend to dope fiend. When someone knows how to tattoo and his tattoo gun and ink supply are up and running, people line up to get tattoo work done—the same gun, ink, and needle for anyone that uses him.

Very few have the time, care, or thought to clean or prepare anything to help stop the spread of disease. When it's time for someone's dope, tattoos, or homosexual activities, it's time. They can't see or feel the disease for years, but their fix is here now. Almost everyone I have hung around since I've been in prison has or is now hepatitis C positive.

For some people their only way to eat or get anything other than state stuff is to gamble. Gambling is taken seriously and can become very hardcore. There's always something for someone to lose, whether or not they have anything. They might need a new mission boy or want you for sexual purposes. They can always sell you or have you sell yourself to pay off the debt. I've seen people lose their chow hall food for weeks at a time and have to beg others for something off their trays to eat. In every prison I've been to, there have been gambling tables going and bookies taking bets.

Most prisoners are pretenders. They see everyone else around them and decide which look, walk, or swagger they need. They do and say whatever they have to in order to impress or show the other prisoners, staff, and guards that they are good, solid, loyal people who deserve their trust. They will do anything they can to take the eyes off them and place them on someone else, when in fact they are hiding who they really are or just working some kind of hustle. You can never get the truth out of anyone. Everyone plays everyone.

This happens all the time in prison. There are always lies, fights, assaults, sexual adventures, gambling, drugs, hustles, thugs, new prisoners coming, and something going on. There are consequences for your actions whether you get caught or not.

You can never forget where you are or who is around you. There are some very hardcore, sinister prisoners who have been convicted of some of the most evil, horrendous crimes imaginable. You see prisoners working out, laughing, with graying hair and big bellies, just doing their own time, and you think they are these harmless people, but you don't know who they really are. This is a strictly controlled environment, and how someone acts in front of watchful eyes is not always how they will act when the eyes are not watching. You have to be ready for anything at any time. I have seen prisoners' closest friends turn into their worst nightmares.

You have to watch everything about everything around you. Prison is an environment based on patterns. They run meals, recreation, visits, and programs at the same time every day, year after year. If you watch everything around you, you will see that the people around you have certain walks, talks, movements, laughs, ways of dressing, fidgeting, and coughing. They stand in the same spots around the same people. This is important to know. If you want to have a more comfortable life, you have to watch and learn everything. The more you know, the more prepared you will be than the people around you.

Because of my conviction, I was required to spend my first ten years in or around a closed custody facility. The same thing every day, around the same people, makes you see life in a different way. My first few years I was lost and angry, but as prison life kept repeating itself, I started listening instead of arguing and I became thankful for what I was going through.

I wanted to share a few prisoners' stories with you so you can see how different prisoners, with different charges and sentences, have lived their lives. We all have our own prison worlds, depending on where we go and what we have done to get there. A lifer will not live prison life like a thief, and a robber will not live life like a murderer.

I wanted life stories that would tell it like it is, but most prisoners are not the kind to sit around and write things down, and few care to help people understand and learn about this life. They won't take the time or make the effort to do anything that won't benefit them. They need you, and if you don't have anything for them, they will go somewhere else.

The few prisoners I could get were the ones who know what they've been through and are tired of it. They want something else in life and hope to help others. Because of that, their stories are all going to be positive, whereas most prisoners' stories are not.

Introduction

When I was nineteen years old, I was arrested for murder. I had never done hard time before and I was scared—so scared that when the state offered me a plea bargain for ten years, I didn't even consider it. I went to trial and was found guilty of murder in the first degree and sentenced to forty-one years in the Washington State Department of Corrections.

My name is Matt Wright. I was born and raised in Richmond Beach, a suburb of Seattle, Washington. My father is a retired ship captain in the Merchant Marines, and my mother worked as an advocate for the birth-to-three program at the University of Washington. I have two sisters. My little sister, Katie, died in 1997, and my big sister, Theodora, is married with two kids. She owns two restaurants in the area we grew up in. We lived in a nice house in a nice neighborhood.

I always seemed to find problems. Until I came to prison, problems never seemed like that big of a deal. You get in trouble and they call your mom to come get you. I've had many arrests and more than a few convictions. As a juvenile, I was convicted for assault, burglary, robbery, theft, and possession of stolen property. I did not have any adult felony convictions when I was arrested, but I did have arrests for statutory rape and forgery and misdemeanor convictions for assault, harassment, and malicious mischief.

This book is about prison—not about *me* in prison but rather the process and procedures, the differences between different prisons and custody levels, the life here and all the different programs they offer to help you. You don't just sit around working out, playing cards, and watching TV all day.

There are long nights, hollow cells, massive noise, violence, pressure, fear, strip searches, peeing in cups, hearings, transfers, the hole, aggressive homosexuals, predators, prey, gang banging, drug addicts, dope dealing, tattooing, disease, gambling, schooling, trailer visits, family, religious programs, self-help groups, and more.

It's not all bad in prison. There are many good people, good staff, and good programs. Every prison is different.

I have to use me to tell this but it is not about me. I will not build things up, I will not lie, and I will not hide things. I want you to understand and know what prison is. I never knew anyone who had been to prison, I don't think it would have helped me but I wish I had someone or something to tell me what prison is and what prison does.

Prison is not just about you. It affects everyone around you. Your mother, father, brothers, sisters, sons, daughters, nieces, nephews, wife, girlfriends, boyfriends, friends, and anyone who cares about you.

It's very hard for your loved ones, financially and emotionally. The processes they have to go through to visit you is humiliating. They stand in long lines in a crowded room, fill out forms, take off their shoes, shake out their bras, walk through metal detectors, and stand for pat searches. Sometimes a drug sniffing dog puts its nose all over their bodies. The guards are not always nice. It is not fun for your loved ones.

Every prison offers different kinds of school, self-help groups, and family programs. Every prison has different groups, gangs, cliques, drugs, violence, gambling and hardcore living. It's up to you how you want to live in prison and what you want to get out of prison.

You'll find staff that will encourage and help you understand situations in a different way, and you'll find staff that won't care what you do either way. Prison does not stop growing, and there's no time to coddle you. Prison is about you and what you do.

This book is about Washington State prisons, because that's all I know. I know not all prisons are the same, but I think they are similar enough that my story will be relevant to all of them. In this book you will find words and terms that might be different from words you would normally hear or use. Please refer to the glossary if you have any questions.

At the end of this book, five prisoners with different charges and sentences share about their prison lives so you can see how people experience life in prison differently.

Then you will read a story by my little sister, Katie. Katie wrote about how what we do (or are accused of doing) affects the people around us. She gives you a firsthand look at how she was traumatized emotionally and mentally because of my arrest and conviction but also how it made her stronger.

When you read this, please remember that this is prison life, the only adult life I have ever known. These are my years, minute by minute, day by day, month by month. It's what I lived; it's all I know.

Chapter 1

Washington State Corrections Center
The Receiving Units

On March 11, 1994, I was sentenced to four hundred and ninety-four months in prison. After the sentence hearing, the judge asked me if I wanted to waive a thirty-day holding period that newly sentenced state prisoners can use to say goodbye to family and friends before being transferred to state custody. I did.

I have been living on the eleventh floor of the King County jail—in the hole twenty-three hours a day, locked down. The only time I leave my cell is for one hour of recreation in a thirty-foot-by-thirty-foot concrete room with nothing in it. Or I can go to another room, where I shower and use the phone for up to twenty minutes at a time. No matter how hard prison is, I cannot take the hole any longer.

On March 16, a guard comes to my cell, slides a brown paper bag under the door, and says, "Put all your shit in the bag. The state is here to get you." About ten minutes later, two guards open the cuff port to my cell door and tell me to turn around and cuff up. They take me to an elevator that goes to a room with about ten other prisoners and tell us all to get naked and throw our clothes in the bucket. We then walk naked into the next room and line up on the wall. Two other guards in different uniforms are standing there. They go to the first two prisoners and tell them to run their hands through their hair, pulled down their ears, open their mouths, lift up their tongues, lift up their arms, lift their ball sacks, turn around and bend over, spread their butt cheeks, stand up, and show the bottom of their feet. They then go down the line. This is my first strip search of many in the Department of Corrections.

When they're finished with all of us, they throw us a pair of orange coveralls, no underwear, no socks, just the coveralls. We've been standing with our bare feet on the dirty floor through all of this. After we put on the coveralls, they throw us a dirty pair of beat-up orange slippers. We turn and face the wall and they put leg and waist chains on us that attach us to the prisoner standing next to us. We

1

then walk through a hallway to a big garage where a white bus is waiting. There are now two other guards with shotguns. They say, "Ladies, get on at the bus and enjoy the ride. Your new daddies are waiting for you."

The bus is similar to a school bus, except that at the front there is a Plexiglas wall separating us from the guards. There's another Plexiglas cage in the middle, where another guard is sitting. They are armed. The seats are low, and there are little windows high up that we cannot see out of. As there is no bathroom, I could only imagine what I would do if we had to go a long distance.

About an hour later, we arrive at the gates of the Washington State Corrections Center in Shelton, Washington. After going through two gates we stop. A guard opens the door and tells us to get off the bus two at a time, walk into the building, and sit on the bench. Once there, they remove our chains and hand us a sack lunch with one milk, an apple, two pieces of bread, and a slice of ham. One by one, we see a lady who asks us questions like, "Do you have any enemies at this prison? Do you need protective custody? Do you have any medical issues?" They tell anyone who has facial hair to go to the sink and shave. We then take pictures for our prison IDs, which we are told we must wear on our upper-left breast at all times. A couple of population prisoners show up and issue us a pair of blue coveralls, socks, underwear, T-shirt, and shoes while the guards stand by. In the R-units everyone wears coveralls. This whole time we're going back and forth from these benches that have metal fencing around them. It reminds me of dog kennels.

After we are all dressed, a couple of guards come in and tell us to follow them. We walk out and I see these three big cell houses, about a hundred feet tall. They look like they're made from stones, all rough and jagged. We get in front of them and the guards stop. They read out our names and point us to whatever units we are going to.

When I walk into the unit all this noise hits me. It sounds like a gym at a high school pep rally, with loud banging and clanging and water running. There's all this yelling and screaming, and it is hard to hear what is happening. To talk to the person next to you, you have to yell.

I walk to the guard and hand him my ID, and he tells me my tier and cell number. The building is two stories high, with four tiers on each floor. At the end of every tier there is a lockbox that the guards open, pulling a lever down to open the cells. Unless a guard steps onto the tier he can't see what that tier is doing; he can see into your cell only if he is standing in front of it. There are no buttons or intercoms in the cell to press if there is an emergency. If you want something, you have to yell and hope someone hears you above all the other noise. I have to ask around to find where my tier is.

At the front of the tier, I see three naked men showering in an area with three showerheads. There is no curtain or stalls, just a bench to put your stuff on. Anyone who walks by or looks onto the tier can see them.

The tier is roughly seventeen cells long with open bars in front. I see people passing things from cell to cell and standing at the bars, talking and yelling. I think they are watching to see who came off the chain—it kind of makes you feel like fresh meat. When I get to my cell and look in, I see this older black guy, around fifty. I don't really know much about prison, but I've heard a lot of things in jail and I know if I live with a colored person I will have problems.

I walk back down the tier and find a guard. "I think there's a mistake."

"What," he asks?

"There is a black in the cell where I am supposed to go."

"We don't play that here," he tells me.

I go back to my cell and go inside after the guard pulls the lever and my cell door slides open. When the cell bars slam shut, I tell him my name.

He asks, "Are you a rapo?"

"No," I tell him.

"Why are you here?"

"A murder conviction," I say.

Then I show him my judgment and sentence, which shows all my crimes and convictions. He tells me he's been imprisoned since 1967 and that he is here for a parole hearing. I tell him that in jail, everyone says we are not supposed to live with other races. He laughs and says, "Nobody will bother you in my cell." Then he takes out an envelope and says, "Take a look at some of my old cellies. I'm still close with most of them." The pictures are all of white guys with long hair. They look like they are gay.

I ask him when they open doors next and he tells me at dinnertime. We eat at 6:30 AM, 11:30 AM, and 5:00 PM every day. He also says that the shower times and yard/gym rotate every other day from afternoon to evening. I tell him that when we go to dinner I am not coming back. I explain that I don't want to give anyone a reason to talk about me.

The tier porter stops by and tells him they are good to go, and he hands him something. He says, "Don't forget about me," and my cellie tells him to come back in five minutes.

He hands me a pair of fingernail clippers and tells me to watch the tier. I look down the tier using the reflection in the clippers as a mirror.

He pulls down his pants, sits on the toilet, and pulls out a rubber glove fingertip from his ass that looks about four inches long. "Safest place in prison," he says.

He rinses it off in the sink and with his teeth, he unties the knot in the end and I see him take out a small needle.

He asks me if I want a hit. "No thanks," I reply.

"You can go first," he says.

"I'm good," I tell him.

He tells me to keep watching the tier as I see him unwrap the small package the porter gave him. Using a piece of foil, he cooks his dope and draws it into the needle.

With his pants still down, he stands up to the mirror on the wall and shoots the dope into his neck. He sits back down on the toilet and closes his eyes, and I see sweat start to run down his face. A couple of minutes later, he heats up some more and draws it into his needle. Then the porter comes by, and he tells him to put his arm through the bars. He does, and my cellmate shoots him up in his arm. The needle has not been cleaned; the porter doesn't even ask. The porter is all happy and tells him thanks. My cellie's pants are still down. He sits back down on the toilet and draws more into his needle. I ask him, "Aren't you going to clean it?" He tells me he has hepatitis C, so it doesn't matter.

I ask him why the needle is so small, and he tells me it's called a binky. You get whatever needle you can and cut it in half, then tie a piece of dental floss to the middle piece so you can still draw your dope up. He says it is easier to store a smaller needle like this than a full-sized one. I asked him what hepatitis C is, and he says, "Just some blood thing." I find out later that it is an incurable blood disease that can be transferred easily via blood-to-blood contact.

When they let us out for dinner, I find the guard and tell him to find some-place else for me. He does not ask why, just nods and tells me to go eat. When I get back, he tells me I'm going to a different cell.

Going to dinner is a different problem. I don't know anyone and I don't know where to sit. In jail, people say that if you sit at the wrong table it can be bad. When I walk into the chow hall it's all separated; whites on one side, blacks on the other, Indians in the middle, and Mexicans in the front middle. I sit down at a white table that has people close to my age and I don't have any problems. The guards do random pat searches on everyone who leaves the chow hall.

At the other prisons it's not like this, but every time they call a meal in the R-units we have to go whether we are hungry or not. They have a group of guards that walk down the tiers after they call chow and look around the cells. They do random searches daily.

We are locked in our cell at all times except meals, yard/gym, showers, and any call-outs. They count us five times a day—6:00 AM, 10:30 AM, 4:00 PM, 9:00 PM, and 12:00 AM. Everyone must be in their cells for count. From 9:00 PM to 6:00 AM, the entire prison is locked down.

There is nothing in our cells. They give us our state clothes and a bedroll with two sheets, two blankets, a pillow, and a chain bag with toothpaste, toothbrush, soap, plastic comb, and a printout of all our meal times, yard/gym times, and address information. We also get the chain bag that we packed at the county jail. In it, we were allowed to bring any court papers, pictures, and hygiene stuff.

The nights are difficult to get through. A lot of people yell from cell to cell, and you can hear everyone farting, coughing, peeing, praying, mumbling, arguing, moaning, screaming, and sometimes fighting. When punches hit the body they make this dull, hard smacking sound that you never forget. The guards do an hourly tier check, but there is no way for them to sneak up to a cell without you knowing. The guards have these big, noisy key chains that rattle whenever they move, and they have to use them to go through any gate at the front or the back of the tier. The gates squeak and rattle, and their boots make thumping sounds that echo loudly with every step. People always yell out when they are on the tiers. It is like a crypt that echoes all your pain and personal moments.

The next morning they take all the new people to medical to get checked. They ask us some questions and send us back to our cells. When I get back, there is a slip on my bed that says all the new prisoners on the chain are to report to some room when yard is called. When we get to this room, they tell us we have to take some tests so they can figure out what they think the best programs for us would be, based on our schooling levels, awareness, and IQ. It takes us about two hours to do all the testing. Everyone is pat searched going into and leaving the school and medical floor.

I get my first shower that night. It is hard showering in front of strangers. It is also very dirty. The showerheads are so close together that the water from our showers splashes all over us; there is no way around it. The walls and floor are grossly stained with filth. I hope it is not like this at all the prisons; I don't want to get used to this. We get showers every other day.

We get to go to the gym today, which looks just like any school gym. They have a schedule for the games—volleyball today, basketball tomorrow, handball after that. Everyone is raced and aged off, just like at the chow hall. I don't see young prisoners hanging out with older ones. They have a room where you can check out things like jump ropes and basketballs. There is no door on the hinges so the guards can see in if they walk by. I look over and see two blacks fighting.

There are phones in the yard and gym. We can only use them during recreation, so there are long lines. Some prisoners' hustle is hanging around the phones selling three-way phone calls. If your family cannot accept collect calls, these guys will call their family and connect the call to your family for some store or favors.

If you have someone on the outside who will send you money, they can do that. All they have to do is buy a money order and mail it to you. All your mail must have your name and Department of Corrections (DOC) number on it.

The next day I see a classification counselor. He asks me which prison I want to go to, and I tell him Twin Rivers. He laughs at me and says that with a first-degree murder conviction I have to do five years closed custody. I asked what closed custody is, and he tells me there are three levels for the prison population. Closed custody is for violent offenders and troublemakers. Medium custody is for long-term violent offenders that stay out of trouble and short-timers with a little trouble. Minimum custody is for the goodie-goodies. He says no matter what I do, I cannot have minimum until four years from my release date, per policy. He says I can go to only three prisons until I am minimum—Washington State Penitentiary (Walla Walla), Clallam Bay Corrections Center (CBCC), and the Washington State Reformatory (WSR).

He says I will have a classification review every year to see how I have been doing and what I've been up to. Once I get my medium custody, I can then ask for a transfer if I want. The custody levels work on a point system, from zero to sixty-seven, with sixty-seven being the best. I ask how many points I have, and he says none. I can't have any points for five years.

The only closed custody prisons are Clallam Bay and Walla Walla. The other prisoners tell me that Walla Walla is where the older prisoners with a lot of time go, and it's calmer. Clallam Bay has a younger population that is more loud and excited. I ask to go to Walla Walla, thinking that if I am around older prisoners I won't have as many problems.

Talking with other prisoners, I start to learn more about the point and classification system. The points go like this:

- Zero to 39: closed custody

- 40 to 54: medium custody

- 55 to 67: minimum

Everything is based on this point system. You can earn one point a month for programming at least fifteen hours a week. You lose one a month for not programming or more for committing infractions. Every major infraction has a set amount of points you can lose. After you lose these points, you can earn them back after being infraction free for a set amount of time.

For the classification system you come to the R-units. Your counselor looks at your charge, age, infraction record, education level, mental health, and physical state and determines what custody you start at. After you get a custody level, they tell you what prisons will accept you, and you can ask for one. After that, if you have more than five years to serve, you get a review every year (if you have fewer than five years you get one every six months). At your review, depending on your custody status, you can ask for a transfer or better privileges.

The counselor tells me that the receiving units are split up into different levels. R-1, R-2, and R-3 are classification units, and once you are classified to go somewhere you will move to R-4 or R-5 and wait for a transfer. Six weeks later, I get my classification papers back and I'm going to Clallam Bay. The next morning I am told to throw all my bedding on the tier and grab my stuff, and a guard walks me over to R-4.

R-4 and R-5 are on the other side of the prison. It's different from the other side, because it's all on one level. There are four wings with a guard booth in the middle. Each wing has a dayroom with tables and showers. Instead of bars, the cells have sliding steel doors with small windows.

When we walk in, the guard lines us all up and tells us where we live is where we live; he's not gonna play the race game. He'll try to keep things calm, but where we are going is where we will be. Any complaints can be told to the hearing officer in the hole. He then gives us our cell assignments. Walking to my cell, I have to stop at the locked door to the dayroom. After taking his time, the guard pops the locked door from the booth and I go in. I know this will happen a lot. I walk into a dayroom with some card tables, three showers on one side, a row of barred windows with books on the ledge, and a long hallway with steel doors on both sides. With doors in the front of the cells, the hallway is dark, gloomy, hollow, and cold. The other prisoners look through their door windows to see the new people. Everyone is always watching everyone.

It's quieter in the cells here, but people still yell loudly from cell to cell. Because there are no bars, if you want to pass things, you have to tie together strips of sheets or elastic from your underwear to make ropes and slide them under your door cracks to other doors. This is called fishing.

They have a speaker built into the wall with a button you can push to listen to the radio. Whoever is working in the guard booth picks the station and the volume level. Sometimes it gets loud, and it's annoying listening to the same station over and over. Even if you turn it off you can still hear all the radios in your neighbors' cells or the cells down the tier.

The chow hall is the same. People still eat with their own race, but they also eat with other prisoners with similar crimes and sentences. Murderers eat with murderers, lifers with lifers; people with short time eat with people with short time. They have tables that are right at the front of the chow hall, where the guards stand and watch us eat, and that's where the sex offenders, rats, and weak people sit. We get only twenty minutes to eat.

Sex offenders, snitches, and the weak live a different prison life than most. They are always the first targets that the prison population go to for their anger or needs. In the back of their minds, they know that at any time they can be attacked or pressured, so they always try to keep themselves within eyesight of the guards and out of sight of the other prisoners. By being as close to the guards as possible, they hope that when something does happen, the guards can get there faster.

The prison population has its own set of rules that everyone is supposed to live by. The words punk and bitch have their own set of rules attached to them. They say that if someone calls you a punk or a bitch, you must fight immediately. You don't wait to go into a cell or a blind spot; no matter where or what the situation is, you fight. If you don't fight or if you show any weakness, you will be treated like a punk or a bitch. In prison, you can treat a punk or a bitch any way you want and they will accept it.

How people see you and how you react to situations is how you'll be treated and remembered. The smallest word can haunt you for a lifetime. Everything is being watched and listened to and the population can't wait for someone to focus on. One man's misery is another man's glory, and fear becomes someone's home. There is no forgiveness here, just actions and consequences.

We get more recreation here, gym in the morning and yard in afternoon for an hour each. It is a different yard and gym than the other units use. The gym has the same stuff, except they have free weights. The yard has a track, soccer, and softball field, dip and pull-up bars, tables and phones.

All the prisoners are grouped together, like in the chow hall. You see some bounce around, hanging out here or there, but not many. I don't see a lot of the people who eat by the guards; they mostly stay in their cells. The sex offenders and weaker prisoners are afraid of all the other prisoners and limit the time they are out of their cell to limit their chances of being assaulted.

We also can start ordering store. You fill out a slip and turn it in by a certain date and a few days later, if you have the money you'll get the store. The store list is not long, but they have most things a prisoner needs: shampoo, soap, toothpaste, deodorant, chips, drinks, candy, fingernail clippers, etc.

There's a stand at the front of unit that holds different forms we might need. Store slips, visiting applications, kites (kites are request forms you can send to staff, medical, and counselors), and money transfer slips (for postage or sending money to someone from your account).

It takes about a month to get my family approved to visit. I mailed the visit applications to them, they filled them out and returned them, and I waited for the prison to approve them. The visits are one hour long and behind glass only. The visits are not nice. The visiting booths accommodate one visitor at a time. It is a small room made of concrete and steel with a fixed stool and desk. There is writing scratched into the Plexiglas and written on the walls. It is cold and dull.

Every night after showers, the tier porters sweep up and pick up all the clothes and trash that gets thrown on the tier. The guards then hand them a stack of brown paper bags with names and prisons written on them. These are passed out to the prisoners who are transferring, and they have about ten minutes to put whatever they want to transfer with inside them.

During your stay in the R-units, if you didn't come with your paperwork you should get a copy of your judgment and sentence as soon as possible so you have it when you get to your next prison. All you have to do is write a kite to the prison records department and they will send you one. Depending on where you're going, it can be very important.

It takes me about eight weeks to get my bag. I fill it up and bring it down to the dayroom to be inventoried by the guards and placed in a cart for the chain bus in the morning.

Before the 6:00 AM count the next morning, I get woken up and told that I have five minutes to get ready and when my door opens I need to be in the dayroom.

When everyone that is leaving is in the dayroom, we get escorted back to where we originally arrived and given a sack lunch. It is the same sack lunch we got last time, an apple, milk, two pieces of bread, and a slice of ham.

After we eat, the guards do the 6:00 AM count, take us out of the cage and strip-search us, and give us a pair of orange coveralls and slippers. We then get leg irons and waist chains placed on us and we're chained to the prisoner next to us. I make sure I am by someone I think I can get along with.

Because there is more than one chain bus leaving, I am placed in a cage with others going to Clallam Bay. We are chained up and escorted onto the bus. The guards take a break, and then we leave for Clallam Bay.

Every prisoner that transfers from one prison to another goes through the R-units. They are horribly overcrowded at all times. Most of the cells in R-4 and R-5 have a person living on the floor. The place is run down and filthy. With all the people moving through, there's no way to stop the spread of disease and clean properly.

There are no programs there. There are books, the radio, yard/gym, and cell time. Everyone does the same thing every day at the same time. It is very easy to have problems. The R-units are the worst place to do prison time.

In talking with other prisoners, I keep getting reminded that I have forty years to do. What I do today can affect me tomorrow. I have to make it through today before I make it through tomorrow. I know this is true—prisoners with my type of sentence are not going anywhere, and I will be around them until I leave.

Chapter 2

Clallam Bay Corrections Center

The bus ride from Shelton to Clallam Bay is about five hours. With your chains on and all the twists and turns, it is not a comfortable ride. This chain bus has a toilet for pissing, but with your hands chained to your waist and you being to another prisoner, it is hard to use.

When we get to Clallam Bay, we go through two gates and park. We all get off the bus and walk into a room with a long bench. They take off our chains and walk us over to the clothing room, where we are issued our state clothing, bedding, and a state chain bag. We don't get coveralls here. For our state clothing, we get three pair of brown pants, five T-shirts, five underwear, five socks, a pair of shoes, and our shower sandals. They tell us our personal chain bags will be issued through the property room when they have time.

The prison is surrounded by guard towers and two fences about fifteen feet high. They have barbwire coils all along the top. The two fences are about twenty feet apart and filled with barbwire coils from fence to fence about ten feet deep.

There are four closed custody units, two on either end of the compound. Connecting the two closed custody units is a wing with the hole (segregation), IMU (long-term segregation), and administration offices. In front of them is a long two-story building with the property room, three chow halls, the chapel, medical, kitchen, visiting room, clothing room, laundry room, law and regular library, and the school floor. There is a grass yard in between the support building and the units. Unless we're at the yard or gym or the medium/minimum custody building, we are surrounded by walls of buildings that are surrounded by a wall of barbwire fences.

There's another building, outside the walls of closed custody, that has four medium and minimum custody units. It is two stories high with two units on each story. The medium prisoners are mostly long-term prisoners who have their points and are waiting to transfer somewhere else. The minimum custody prisoners are here to do the jobs that the prison needs, like go outside the gates to mow lawns or clean parking lots, which the other prisoners cannot do. They have their own chow hall and they go to yard and gym at different times than we do in closed custody. We don't see them much.

After we get changed we are told to go to C-unit. When I walk outside, I see two big, round units to my left and two to my right. There's a long level unit between them, connecting the two. Walking into C-unit there is a rotunda with a guard booth in the middle. There is a guard's office next to the door where we come in. The rotunda has three different color pods (red, brown, and green) surrounding it. The pods all have Plexiglas fronts so the guard booth can see the dayrooms and all the cell doors. Many of the prisoners are lined up at the glass watching the ducks (new prisoners) arrive.

The guard in the booth tells us our cell assignments and instructs us to go to green pod. That's where they put the new prisoners until they see a counselor, who decides what unit we need to go to. The prisoners call it the duck pod. On my way in, I see two guys in brown pod kissing.

The pods are three tiers high, eleven cells along. There is a spiral staircase in the middle of the pods leading to the tiers but also acting as a fence the divides the dayroom in half. On each side of the dayroom there are three steel tables with five stools that don't move. The blacks sit on one side and the whites sit on the other. The Mexicans and Indians hang out around both sides wherever there is an open table.

The cells are nice. There is a door, two bunks, a desk and stool, toilet and sink. There is a small window you can see out of. You can only leave your cell during a ten-minute gate that they run at the top of every hour or at chow. You have a button to push to open the doors, which only works during gates or chow. If you push the button when it is not gate time, the guard will come to your cell, and if it's not a medical emergency, you will get infracted. If you're out of your cell you can stay out, but if you are in your cell you have to wait. The cells are small but comfortable. To get in your cell, you stand at the door, and when the guard in the booth feels like it, he will pop the lock open. Everyone here has his own cell.

When I get settled in my cell I look in the chain bag they gave me. There's a packet from the school floor telling us about their classes and a packet telling us about all the jobs available. It says that you have to program at least fifteen hours a week through school or work or you are locked in your cell from 8:00 AM to 4:00 PM every day. There's a list of visiting room rules and personal property we are allowed. They also have a schedule for the law and regular library and rules. The library is open five days a week at different times of the day. All units go at different times.

From 9:00 PM to 6:00 AM everyone is locked in his cell. Other than that, there's a lot of freedom. There are showers and phones at the end of all the tiers. The dayroom is open at all times except during counts, which are 11:00 AM and 4:00 PM and the 9:00 PM to 6:00 AM lockdown. You have yard or gym in the morning and night one day, in the afternoon the next day. If you want, you can sit in the dayroom, talk on the phone, shower, and use the yard or gym a total of nine hours a day.

There are four closed custody units, A & B and C & D. A & B and C & D have separate chow halls. The medium and minimum custody building has its own chow hall. The units and pods rotate to determine who goes to chow first and in what order. They don't run the duck pod for chow until all the other units have eaten. Many violent incidents happen in the chow hall over seats, and they want to give you a chance to find your way.

The yard and gym are like the R-units, except that the yard has tennis, pickle ball, and basketball courts. You are pat searched by a guard whenever you leave the yard or gym.

I don't see a counselor or anything, but three days after I get here I am sent from the duck pod to B-unit red pod. I get there during recreation time, and most people are gone, but there are four black guys playing cards in the dayroom. I go to my cell to put my stuff away and make my bed when one of them comes to my door and tells me to come out. He asks if I have paperwork. I tell him that I haven't gotten my personal chain bag yet, but I was told that as soon as I got a cell I would be called out to get it. He says, "Everyone gets a day or two, but anyone that doesn't have it will not stay on mainline," and he walks off.

After the 11:00 AM count clears, they call chow, all meals are optional here. I don't know anyone, and no one is talking to me yet (because I do not have my paperwork). It's very intimidating and scary walking into the chow hall alone. When I walk in it is all raced off. I instantly see the ding and rapo table (a ding is a medicated or mentally disabled individual). At least I know where not to go.

I get my tray and walk over to a table with some dudes my age. A guy says, "Table's full." I turn to the table next to it and they say the same thing. There is only one guy sitting at another table so I sit down there. He says, "Table's full." I tell him I will be fast, but I just can't keep walking around. I finish and go back to the unit. During dinner, the same stuff happens, so I go to the same table as lunch. This time he doesn't say anything.

It is very hard to get a seat in the chow hall. All the prisoners have their own clique or group that they hang around, and they only eat with each other, so if you don't know someone or you aren't cliqued up, you don't eat. I have seen people get their tray and walk over to where we put our trays when we are done eating and stand there and cram as much food into their mouths as they can, meal after meal, until the guards come by and tell them to leave.

Once you start sitting at a table and get a seat, it is your responsibility to protect your table. Other races and cliques are always looking to expand and to take tables. Everyone knows who sits where, and if you do not do everything you can to protect your table, you will go hungry. Where you sit determines how you will be seen and treated. I have seen stabbings, beatings, hot coffee thrown in people's faces, and the whole chow hall erupt in a violent brawl over someone sitting in the wrong seat.

That night I checked out the cleaning gear to clean my cell. When I start to mop my cell floor, someone runs into my cell and I get punched in the back of the head. We start fighting and I see that it is the same guy from the chow hall. It's an okay fight for both of us. Someone closed the door when he came in, so after the fight we have to wait for the next gate for him to leave. We start talking and telling each other why we are here and after a little while he says, "You can keep sitting at our table." I sat in the same seat until I transferred out four years later.

The first thing you learn when you get here is that everybody hates sex offenders, rats, girly homosexuals and weak people. They are picked on, assaulted, and preyed upon. If they stay in population, it's because the other prisoners don't know about them yet or they are there as someone's toy or amusement. The guards hate them as much as everyone else.

Not all sex offenders, rats, and homosexuals are treated the same. There are many prisoners with bad charges or who did questionable stuff to the wrong people in the past, and there are many homosexuals who either keep their business private or within their cliques. They know how to carry themselves. Others are violent hardcore prisoners who not only live problem free but also thrive in the population. Many prisoners know and talk about them, but very few say things to their faces. But mostly, an individual who has sex offences, has done or said the wrong things in the past, or is openly gay has a very hard prison life. They usually get the worst of everything and are always expecting anything.

Within these cliques there is a further hierarchy of status and order. Lifers and murderers are mostly looked up to by the other prisoners for answers, decisions, and direction. They get the best tables in the chow hall, the best jobs, the best cells to live in, and the most respect. If you are not going home or your release date is decades away, you will do things that others are scared to do or won't do.

Most cliques, groups, and gangs have someone that others look up to and go to for advice, representation, and direction. They're called "heads" or "shot callers." If you have a problem with someone in a clique, and it doesn't need to be dealt with immediately, you go to a shot caller first and let him know what's going on so the problem can be squashed or dealt with between you two and not others. If the person you are having a problem with is part of a clique and you do something without talking to the shot caller, it could lead to many other problems, because the clique might want to set an example or save face. The shot caller has to be able to keep his clique in order because everyone is watching, and if he can't, someone will take his place. How the prison population acts mostly depends on how hardcore the shot callers are. Everyone has to live how everyone else is living.

A cell is not just a cell; it becomes your home, and you want to live as comfortably as you can. You have end cells, top cells, good view cells, etc. You can move around or swap cells anytime you want. I have heard of people "buying" cells from people for several hundred dollars, fighting, stabbing, threatening, and doing whatever it takes to get a good cell. That is how serious some people take it. All cells are searched randomly once a month by two guards.

In cell searches at most prisons, two guards will come to your cell, ask you to step out, pat search you, and tell you to go wait in the dayroom. If you are not home, they just go in and search the cell. They are usually respectful with your stuff and just go in and move things around and search. Most cell searches are done in the morning and afternoon.

You are allowed a lot of personal property. Two pairs of pants, six T-shirts, three dress shirts, two pairs of shorts, two sweatpants, two sweatshirts, six pairs of socks, a sweater, and a lot of other little stuff. The prison store sells stuff besides food—radios, TVs, cups, bowls, stingers (used to boil water in your cell), fingernail clippers, headphones, and other little stuff. You can buy it off your account from the store or an outside vendor or have family or friends mail it in. You are allowed only four packages a year, one every three months. You can get really comfortable if you save your paychecks or your loved ones helps you out with money.

I bought my TV and radio about two weeks after I got here. My whole world changed—I now had something to look forward to, a reason to cell in and forget about the prison politics and pass the time half enjoyably.

My sisters mailed me a clothing package. To receive any store-bought property, you have to wait for the property room to process your stuff and either engrave it or stamp it with your DOC number. Then they add it to your property matrix and call you there to issue you whatever you got. Sometimes it is fast, sometimes it is not, but it is nice to have my own things.

Everyone is cliqued up. Even the cliques have cliques. In the chow halls, you don't just have things raced off. There are the gangs, lifers, murderers, dope fiends, weight lifters, thugs, old timers, bikers, sex offenders, and dings. They all eat together, live together, stay together, and think together.

I don't want to join a clique. When you clique up, you take on other people's responsibilities and problems. If they fight, you fight. If they hate, you hate. It can be helpful, but it is also a curse. I don't fit in with these people. I'm not in any of the cliques. I'm a suburban white kid who grew up in the nineties. This is like the sixties.

Even though I don't want to hang out with the people at my table, sitting there is a responsibility. We walk to chow together, leave chow together, and do not let others sit at or attack our table. You have to be able to know that when you are eating, someone is looking over your shoulder.

Slowly I start to find other people like me. As people go to the hole or transfer and spots open up, I bring them to the table.

The hole is where they place you away from the general population for infractions, administrative segregation, or protective custody. It is twenty-three-hour-a-day lockdown, where you are not in physical contact with other prisoners and you get out of your cell only one hour a day to shower, use the phone, or take recreation. You are allowed only books and mail in the cells.

There are three ways you can be removed from population and placed in the hole.

1. *Disciplinary segregation* occurs when you get an infraction for something and they place you in the hole pending a punishment hearing, or you go to an infraction hearing and they sentence you to hole time (you don't go to the hole for all infractions).

2. *Administrative segregation* is when the staff places you in the hole for some kind of investigation. An investigation can include posing a security threat, causing yourself harm, acting as a confidential informant, and trying to escape. The investigation cannot last more than eighty-four days before they must release you to population or place you in the Intensive Management Unit (IMU) for a program. A program is the same as the hole, but you have a level system that lets you earn stuff like store, magazines, newspapers, radios, and TVs. An IMU program usually lasts less than a couple of years.

3. *Protective custody* is for any prisoner in population who feels threatened, pressured, assaulted, or intimidated and needs protection. The prison staff can place you in protective custody if they feel you need it. They do not have a special place for protective custody prisoners. They are placed in the hole and stay there until they ask to go back to population, are sent back to population by the administration, or are transferred to another prison.

People go to and from the hole daily, and there's always something going on. No matter what you do here, you're always going to come back from the hole. Closed custody is the end of the road—there's no place else to send you. How you live here is how they will see you here. Everything happens faster and harder here than anywhere else. It's weird, because people act one way when certain people are around and another way when others are around. Since people are always coming and going, it is never the same. What you laugh about today, you fight about tomorrow.

It's hard to describe how serious things are here. People keep coming by my cell asking to read my paperwork. Everyone is always watching everyone and pointing out how they think things are or how you are handling your situation or how they should have been handled differently. There is no slack. Everything is analyzed.

Finally, a guy comes by my cell and asks to see my paperwork.

"I will bring it out to the dayroom. Go get yours," I say. He looks at me weird and starts telling people "paperwork party." The word spreads quickly, and soon everyone is in the dayroom with his paperwork. Since I was the one that called it, it is my responsibility to deal with anyone that produces odd paperwork or questions why he should show his. I ended up fighting someone in my cell.

In the morning and afternoon the dayroom is packed, but it is quieter and more on edge, because prisoners are watching for things and have to be ready to fight for whatever they are watching out for. People play cards and talk, but when the guards move everything gets serious. If they try to come in for a tier check, they yell out. This is when people put their work in. They are getting high with each other, tattooing and fighting in the cells, and they need lookouts. They can't do it in the evening, because so many serious incidents happen that we get celled in early all the time. Nobody wants to get caught somewhere he is not supposed to be.

I get called down to the school floor and told that if I don't have my high school diploma I have to get my GED before I can work or do other schooling. I enroll in school and get my GED about six weeks later.

They have a lot of good classes and programs here. Electronics Repair, Keyboarding, Intro to Windows 95, Writing, and Math, among others. They also have self-help groups like anger management, parenting, job readiness, chemical dependency, and religious studies. All prisoners go through a metal detector and are pat searched when leaving the school floor.

Prisoners are often forced into schooling or work when they don't want to be there. Since they are forced to be there, they want everyone to know they were forced and this makes it hard for the people who want to be there.

A week after I came here I got my first visit. You have contact visits here. I have not been touched by family in over a year. The visit room is very nice. There are tables and chairs, carpet on the floor, vending machines so our visitors can bring in money and buy us food, candy, and drinks. They have microwaves to cook with. The visiting hours are from 10:00 AM to 8:00 PM, five days a week. Your family shows up during the visiting hours, shows the staff their IDs, and they can walk into the visit room. Once they are approved at an institution, they are approved at all institutions, unless you take them off your visit list or they request to be removed from it.

All prisoners are pat searched on the way into the visits and strip-searched on the way out. You are allowed to wear your personal clothes.

The visits have meant a lot to me. I was too young to really talk with my family when I was free, but now we get nice peaceful time together where we can relax and talk. My family drives up twice a week, four hours each way.

They have trailer visits for your immediate family here. I finally see my counselor after I write a kite asking how to apply. I get the forms and send them to my family, but before I can get approved, another prisoner at a trailer visit with his wife gets into a fight with her and stabs her. She runs outside for help and he follows, stabbing her until the guard in the tower looking over the trailers shoots him. They both live, but closed custody prisoners can no longer have trailer visits.

They have a bulletin board in every pod's dayroom. Every day, they post a daily callout sheet on all the pod bulletin boards for any medical, dental, property, chapel, grievance, work and other appointments you might have. If you miss a callout you can be infracted.

If you have any medical, mental health, or dental problems, every morning after breakfast they have sick call where you can go to the medical floor to see a nurse and tell him or her your problem. If it's important, you will be seen then, or you leave and will be placed on the callout to see someone within a few days.

Anytime you go to the medical floor you have to check in at a guard booth, wait for a door to be opened, walk up some stairs, wait for another door to be opened, check in with another guard booth, and wait in the waiting area to be called out. You are pat searched on the way in and out.

If you have an issue with something or someone on the prison staff, there is a grievance process. You fill out a form and turn it into a box. The grievance coordinator investigates, and a few days later you are called out to talk to the grievance coordinator. I don't file any complaints, because I know I'll never get the response I want and might even be retaliated against.

They have chapel programs for anyone who wants to go. There are different services and programs daily. You have to write a kite to be placed on the callout to attend.

The barbershop is across from the unit office. They allow the barber to have a comb and hair clippers, no scissors. You have to send a kite to the guard's office requesting a haircut appointment and they will send you notice of the day and time. If you do not show up, you cannot get a haircut for thirty days.

You have to wait for everything here. To leave the pod you go to the door and push a button. The guard will ask you what you want. When you tell him, he will look around, check callouts, make a phone call, and then ask again what you want. Then he will pop the door lock, and when you walk to the unit's front door, he will ask everything all over again. To walk a hundred feet, you will be asked once or twice what you're doing or get pat searched here and walk ten feet and get pat searched there. It is very frustrating and annoying.

The guards come around to your cell after the 4:00 PM count and slide any mail you might have under your door. You are allowed to have letters, pictures, and drawings. You may purchase or have your loved ones order you most newspapers, magazines, catalogs, and books.

I start learning how to play cards, and most games are fun, but I realize fast that prisoners don't play cards for fun. There are people here who make their living by playing cards and they're always looking for some new sucker to feed them. It's also a way to get people to do stuff for you. Get them into debt and tell them if they want to clear it up they have to assault someone, run into someone's cell and smash his stuff, bring in dope through the visit room, do sexual favors for him or his buddies, etc.

I am lucky to have a family that cares about me and supports me. I never knew how serious a few dollars could be, I learned a lot by playing cards.

As I get to know about the cliques, I see that most cliques don't go along with others. They're always preying on each other, but they need each other to keep themselves strong. As much as they hate each other, they also have respect for each other. If a clique has a problem with someone in a pod they're not in, they might ask another clique to deal with him. Favors go back and forth.

This guy moved to our pod from a different unit. Someone somewhere asks for a favor. This guy is fortyish, with an average build and glasses. As he waits for dinner in the dayroom, another dude gives a nod to the other prisoners and they form a wall in front of the window so the guards can't see, and he starts beating him. Other prisoners kick and punch him whenever he gets close to them. As he lies on the ground bleeding, everyone starts to walk away, because when the guards see him they don't want to be close. His glasses are lying next to him, and as everyone starts to walk away, I see someone stomp on them and laugh.

There are many drugs in prison. Anyone that can get them is very powerful. They come in through the visit room, guards or other staff, packages, or mail.

There's a guy that bought some dope and his money was a couple of days late. The dope man has to make an example, or everyone will not pay or be late. He gives another guy dope and that guy goes into the late man's cell and smashes his TV and radio, pours bleach all over his personal clothes, and shits on his bed.

Prisoners get beaten, stabbed, forced to do things they don't want to, and sexually assaulted over drugs. Being a dope fiend in prison can be a very hard life.

There are many guards who do their jobs and go home. You can't blame them for doing their jobs. But you also have guards who like to push buttons and amuse themselves. They play games, talk down to us, search our cells wrong, or write up silly infractions. Some just won't leave you alone. This sometimes causes violence besides the violence we create for ourselves.

There are speakers in the ceiling of the pods so the guards can call chow, announce visits, tell us to calm down, whatever the guards need to say. There's this one guard who works in the booth who always turns the volume of the speaker all the way up. It gets everyone riled up and drives us crazy. Prisoners always yell at him to knock it off and he just smiles.

This one prisoner has a thirty-year sentence and is HIV positive. He is tired of taking this guard's crap, so he bites is tongue and when the guard comes into the pod for a tier check, he spits blood into the guard's eyes and starts beating him.

For a lot of us this is our home. We don't have anything but this and each other. We might not get along, and we might attack each other, but for some things it's us against them. We don't have anything better to do than sit around and talk, plan, and conspire to make things better and amuse ourselves.

There are two kinds of infractions, majors and minors. A major infraction can have segregation time as punishment. A minor infraction has nonsegregation time, such as cell confinement.

When you get a major infraction, you get a hearing and a chance to explain the situation. The hearing officer then decides your guilt or innocence and any punishment.

If you get a major infraction and you go to the hole, a few days later you'll get a copy of the infraction and then have a hearing. For major infractions that they don't take you to the hole, when the infraction is written they call you to the booth and serve you with it. You then get a hearing in a few days.

For my first major infraction, I was called to the booth and served with the infraction. A few days later, I went to my hearing and was found guilty and sentenced to five days in the hole.

I was cuffed up from behind and walked over to segregation. I was placed in a little room, strip-searched, and given a T-shirt, underwear, socks, coveralls, and slippers. I was then taken to my cell. My cell had a mattress with a bedroll and paper bag on top of it. In the bag was toothpaste, toothbrush, and a comb. There were two books on the desk. (They do book exchange twice a week.) It is twenty-three hours a day lockdown, and when you get your hour out, it is either in a

Plexiglas fifteen-by-fifteen-foot enclosed dayroom with only a phone or a twenty-by-twenty-foot walled-off room outside with a phone, dip bars, and pull-up bars.

The hole can do weird things to people's minds. Some work out in their cells, sleep, and read the time away, and others lose it. They mutilate their bodies by cutting off their penises and balls, gouging out their eyes, eating their flesh, clawing their fingers to the bone, rubbing shit all over themselves. They bang on the walls, flood their cells, scream and shout, assault the guards by throwing shit and piss cocktails on them or grabbing and biting or stabbing them through the cuff ports (all doors have cuff ports so the guards can cuff us up and feed us). Some do things hoping to get out of the hole and sent to a medical or psych ward. Others are mentally ill, but I think most just don't know how to be alone or aren't strong enough to beat the solitude.

Whenever a serious incident happens, the prison places general population on a lockdown to investigate. In a lockdown, we're locked in our cells twenty-four hours a day until whatever they are investigating ends. You don't get visits, phone calls, showers, or any recreation time. They bring your meals and any cell supplies you might need to your cell. Usually the lockdown lasts a day or two, but I have been on one that lasted fourteen days and others a week are so. If they do last that long, they find ways to squeeze us out for showers.

In 1997, my sister Katie died. I was called to the unit's sergeant's office and told, then allowed to call my family. The next morning my counselor called me into her office and told me if I wanted to, I could go to the funeral.

I was allowed to wear my own clothes to the funeral, but I had waist restraints and shackles placed on me. I was transported in a Suburban by two guards who treated me good and were cool about everything. When we got there, they looked around and saw the surrounding area and told me if I gave them my word I wouldn't do anything stupid they would crawl off into a corner. I give them my word and it was a nice funeral for my family and me. I will always be thankful.

The day after I got back I am called to my counselor's office and told that the policy for first-degree murder has changed and now I have to do only four years closed custody instead of five. She then tells me if I stay out of trouble until my next yearly review, she will have me transferred to the Washington State Reformatory. The reformatory is about a thirty-minute drive for my family. I don't tell any other prisoners what she said, because I don't want anyone to try and ruin it for me.

For every yearly review you have, there's a counselor, custody unit supervisor (CUS), and the sergeant present. After they all ask whatever they want to ask and your review is over, the unit team signs your yearly review paperwork and it gets sent to the custody program manager (CPM) and then the superintendent. If they all agree and sign off, then whatever the unit team recommends will happen. It usually takes six weeks for your review paperwork to go through the process, and you get a copy back in the mail.

I don't see the unit staff that often. Once a year, I get my yearly review and they ask how things are and what I've been doing, but since I can't go anywhere and don't really need anything, that's it. I go to this review and it is different. My counselor asks that I be transferred and I am promoted to medium custody. I will be sent to the medium part of the prison's building to wait for a transfer to the Washington State Reformatory (WSR).

I've been in closed custody my whole time here. I am excited that visiting will be better for my family, but I don't know anything about WSR or the building. I have built up relationships here and I am comfortable, but I'll have to start over. I don't know what to expect. It is a hard decision for me not to do something that will give me another infraction to keep myself in closed custody. I didn't think I would get approved for a transfer.

About two weeks later, I pack up and move to the building's J-unit. The building is similar to closed custody. You are at a different custody level, but you are still around closed custody. For me it's more like a demotion, because I have gone from a single cell with my own toilet to a two-man cell with a community toilet, and the attitudes and politics are the same.

Seeing all the faces here is like a neighborhood reunion. They throw you in a cell with someone of your race when you get there, but you can move to other cells if you find someone you want to live with. I don't have to look for a seat in the chow hall.

When you leave for a transfer, you're allowed to bring two boxes of personal property with you on the chain bus. The rest of your personal property gets sent through the mail, and you never know how long it takes to get shipped. In my chain boxes, I pack some store, shorts, shoes, hygiene stuff, bowl, stinger, my judgment and sentence, and so on.

Ten weeks after I get to the building, I'm told to box my property up and bring it to the property room for shipment to WSR. I leave the next morning.

Every prison's chain bus goes to and from Shelton on a particular day. Clallam Bay's is Wednesday, Walla Walla's is Thursday, and WSR's is Monday. I go to the R-units on a Wednesday and leave for WSR on a Monday, five days later.

Chapter 3

Washington State Reformatory

Nothing has changed in the R-units since I last left. I get the same snack lunch that I got when I left: an apple, milk, two pieces of bread, and a slice of ham. It is still filthy, overcrowded, and noisy. It's a lot harder coming through here this time; I'm used to having my own place and my neighbors treating me how they want to be treated.

The chain ride from Shelton to the reformatory is about an hour. It isn't too bad of a ride. When we get there, we shuffle off the bus and into a receiving area that has a long bench where we wait to get unchained. After that we have our pictures taken for new IDs, and then we are escorted to C & D units dayroom, where a counselor is waiting to give us an orientation.

When we walk out of receiving, I see that there is a thirty-foot square-shaped wall around the entire prison. There are no fences, just the wall and guard towers. The prison has everything in a towering building that has four units at the front of the prison. The building is cut in half by a long hallway that leads to the main entrance, where visitors and guards enter. On either side of the hallway are two units, one in front of the other, A & B and C & D. They are forty cells long and four tiers high each. At the end of each tier are three showers on one side and the counselor, sergeant, and CUS offices on the other, as well as a personal clothes laundry room. About fifteen feet in front of all the cells is a wall. On the wall across from the first tier is a line of phones down the tier. You can only touch the wall from the first tier. The other tiers all have a three-foot-wide catwalk used to walk up and down the tier. In the middle of the tier is a staircase that leads to all the tiers and the unit's entrance.

Behind the living units is the rest of the main prison. The chow halls are between A & B and C & D. Medical, the visiting room, the clothing room, the property room, administration offices, the hole, and the dayrooms are all between or behind the units, but in the main building.

Outside the main building there's the yard and gym, then a smaller building called the PAB (Public Access Building), which has a law and regular library, band room, and different offices for the prison clubs. There are other office buildings around or behind the gym and PAB that house the chapel, school floors, and different job sites.

At the orientation, the counselor tells us that they will not tolerate serious infractions here. If you get one, you will be transferred. He says they have trailers, good paying jobs, single cells, a visiting room close to the city, different prisoners clubs, and a relaxed population.

He explains the prison's surroundings, its movement schedules, and the open-door policy with its grievance coordinator for anyone who needs help. Also, the chapel is open to all whenever gates are run. They offer different religious services and programs throughout the week if we wish to attend. If you have any medical or dental needs, just write a kite and you'll be called out; for emergencies, tell the guards and you'll be seen immediately. We can shower, use the phone or go to the counselor, CUS, or sergeant's office anytime we want, as long as it is not count time and they are in.

I ask how to get involved in the trailer program. He looks at my ID and says, "Counselors have an open-door policy. Anytime we are here, you're welcome to stop by and talk." He then says to me, "You are on my caseload. After you get to your cell, stop by and I will give you the trailer forms you need." Next he explains to us the jobs, self-help programs, and schooling classes, and he sends us to the clothing room to get our state-issued clothing and bedrolls.

Every time you leave the main building they do random pat searches, and every time you come back in the main building you have to clear a metal detector and get pat searched.

When we get to the clothing room there are a few prisoners standing behind a counter with a chain link fence in front of it. There are no guards or staff. They ask us what size clothes we want and give them to us. At the other prisons, you have staff watching your every move.

The prisoners then give us our cell assignment. The guy telling us looks at me and laughs.

I ask, "What's so funny?"

He says, "You're moving in with Big Phil."

I know this name. He was at Clallam Bay when I first got there, and I have heard all these stories about him being this massive predator of young ones. He is built like a barrel and as strong as they come.

"I thought they are all single cells?"

He says, "They are painting half the units, so everyone is doubled up until they are done."

They have hourly ten-minute gates when we can go to different parts of the prison, such as the yard, gym, chapel, and Public Access Building. You can only visit these places during movement, but you can leave and go back to your cell whenever you want. No matter where you go, unless you have a work assignment, you have to be back in your cells for the 11:00 AM and 4:00 PM counts. The prison is locked down from 9:00 PM to the 6:00 AM count clear.

I find my cell, drop off my stuff, and start asking around for Phil. Someone tells me to look for the biggest white guy in the yard, with a shiny shaved head. I walk out to the yard and he is easy to find. I walk up to him and introduce myself and ask if we can talk privately. I tell him that they threw me in his cell and that I've heard a lot of things about him, and I let him know that I'm not gay and if he doesn't want me there I will refuse to cell in.

He isn't worried about it, he says. I can stay a few days until I find a new cell. I was only there a week, but over the years Phil and I became close friends. I never asked about the stories I heard, but since I've known him he's been nothing but a good person.

The cells here are tiny. They all have bars, two bunks, a desk, shelves, a toilet, and a sink. The bunks have one end that touches the bars and the other end a few inches from the toilet. I sleep with my head opposite the bars, because this is prison and I don't want my neck cut while I am sleeping. The cells are about five feet wide and eight feet long. People are not disrespectful or noisy at night but you can hear all their laughing, farting, coughing, grunting, and so on. All cells are searched once a month by two guards.

Every time they call chow, your cell bars slide open to let you out. You can feel the vibrations of the doors opening and closing for what feels like every minute of every day, and it is very loud. If you're sleeping or at work they still open for chow. For gates, visit, or callouts, when you need to leave your cell, you have a sign with your cell number on it in your cell and you put it through the bars and they will see it and open your cell. There are no buttons or intercoms, just your sign and voice.

I was called to the property room four days after got here to get my personal property. Everything is starting to get comfortable. I didn't want to leave Clallam Bay, but I haven't had any problems and there isn't any stress here. I get my property and set it up and do my program. It's kind of nice. You have to clear a metal detector and get pat searched coming back from the property room.

They have a few prison clubs here—the Lifers, Native Americans, Hispanics, Blacks, Veterans, and a program that brings college students into the prison. The college program is supposed to teach us about life outside of here, and we are supposed to teach them about life in here. The clubs have a lot of power. The prison keeps the leaders of the clubs informed on what they are up to, and the clubs keep the prison informed on what we are up to. They want us to stay as calm as possible, and we want them to keep as steady as possible, so it works out well.

Every night they post the callouts for the next day on the unit bulletin board. It is our responsibility to check it and show up for our callouts, or we can be infracted. The callouts can be for medical, dental, mental health, job, school, property, or other appointments. I have never had a problem getting treated for medical or dental. My only problem is that dental department does not do any teeth cleaning. When you go to and from any appointments on the medical floor, you get pat searched.

After moving out of Phil's cell, I moved in with a guy my age, but I did not like the location of the cell, so I moved in with this other guy, but that cell was not any better. Not long after that, they opened the whole prison up and I got a single cell in a good location.

Even if your neighbors are respectful the noise never goes away. The guards all have institutional radios that are always on, and every time someone calls someone or says something on it, it beeps loudly, then you hear them talking. When they walk around, their keys jingle and the tier gates squeak open or scrape the floor. The unit fans sound like air blowers. During the mornings, afternoons, and evenings, the showers are always on, sounding like a dozen sprinklers going. Everything is concrete and steel, so nothing absorbs the sound. It always sounds hollow, with echoes reverberating off every wall.

The barbershop is across from C & D unit's dayroom. The shop has most barber tools, including scissors. You write a kite and say what time would be best for you to come down, and the barbers schedule you an appointment and send you a slip in the mail.

Five days a week, the guards come around after the 9:00 PM count and pass out mail. You can have pictures, letters, drawings, and purchases you or your loved ones have made, including magazines, newspapers, catalogs, and books.

You can move or swap cells every day if you want, but once you get a cell, unless you want to move it's yours. If you go to the hole, trailers, hospital, or somewhere else, the guards come by and put a chain and a padlock around the bars so the door can't open. People will pay good money for the right location.

The inmates here are mostly long-term prisoners who have earned their points but can't be sent to less secure prisons. Everyone does their own thing here—cliques, gangs, bikers, homosexuals, dope fiends, God freaks, suck asses, weight-lifters—and nobody cares who you are or what you're doing as long as you stay out of their way.

In R-units and Clallam Bay, if something was going on, everyone stopped to see what it is. Here if you stop you might be fighting.

In prison, the manlier homosexuals don't usually have problems, but the feminine homosexuals are always preyed upon. They get sexually assaulted, have their store and property taken, and are talked down to and treated like weaklings. That does not happen as much here. Because this prison is for long-term prisoners and lifers, the homosexuals can excel.

I've seen prisoners wearing makeup and women's clothing, guys selling themselves from cell to cell and getting sold from cell to cell, and even a wedding between two dudes in the yard. I've had homosexuals ask if they can do things for me and I've had love letters placed on my bed when I am not home. It is weird to see them so loud and out when usually they are so quiet and hidden. I always try to be respectful but stern in my responses. I want to be friendly but not weak.

The chow hall is raced off and cliqued off, just like everywhere else. Phil let me sit at his table until I find my own spot. It took me only a day or two. The seats are not as much of a problem in the chow halls here. Everyone has been around and knows the deal, and if they don't and they sit down, you just point them in the direction you think they will fit in and they'll find their way. The guards do random pat searches of prisoners coming to or from the chow hall.

Problems between people here are usually taken care of quietly and privately. Very little violence is seen, but there is always something going on.

I start to get visits as soon as I get here. The visitors' room is as nice as Clallam Bay's, but with better vending machines. There is visiting five days a week, and it is relaxed and comfortable. When they call visits, they announce them over a prison loud speaker system. You hear your name and walk up to the visit room. You're allowed to wear your personal clothes to the visit. Every prisoner gets pat searched going into the visits and strip-searched leaving the visit.

Within a few weeks, I am approved for trailer visits. They have five manufactured homes in the back corner of the prison where our loved ones can come and spend the night with us.

You can have one- or two-day trailers. Your loved ones are allowed to bring in most store-bought foods and drinks, and we do our own cooking. The trailers have household goods like ovens, microwaves, TVs, radios, couches, beds, tables, and plastic silverware. The prison has a tower looking over them, and for counts they call you to wave at it instead of disturbing your family. The trailers are clean and kept up.

They are the best thing for my family relationship I could have. The process for them is easy. The night before you have a trailer, you go to the receiving unit and fill out some forms, get strip-searched, and stand naked and pee in a cup as a guard watches. You have to give a urine sample before and after every trailer visit.

The next afternoon you bring your clothes and stuff you're bringing to the trailer to the receiving unit and have them searched and inventoried, then get strip-searched, dressed and walked out to the trailers. When you leave you get strip-searched in the trailer and walked back to the receiving units, where you get strip-searched again, then pee in a cup while a guard watches, get dressed, and walk back to your unit.

I get called to the kitchen and told that every new prisoner has to do a ninety-day mandatory work assignment in the kitchen. The prisoner clerk that does all the hiring and work assignments tells me he will give me a waiver out of the kitchen if I let him suck my dick. That doesn't bother me; everyone has his own hustle in prison. What bothered me was when I offered to pay for the waiver, he laughed and said, "I only want one thing." I then said some things that I probably shouldn't have, and he said, "I'm telling my daddy."

A prison "daddy" has to take care of his punk or he will find someone who will, but he also is responsible for all of his punk's actions. After I got the job assignment I wanted, I felt it would be best to go to the yard and introduce myself to his daddy.

I know that punks are always dramatizing things, and I want to get this cleared up before it gets too serious. When I find him and let him know what's going on, he tells me that he will have the kitchen clerk stop by my cell and apologize, and if I want to work out a price he will give me a waiver.

The prison daddy has to not only take care of his punks but also discipline him. I think that many punks do stuff on purpose to test the daddies, because they want to feel wanted and loved.

I start work in the kitchen the next day. All state jobs here pay $0.42 an hour. You cannot make more than $52 a month. Every time you go to work or leave work, you get pat searched. They also do random strip searches.

There are three classes of prison job. Class 3 is a state job that pays up to $52 a month (kitchen, porter, recreation, clerk, teacher's assistant, etc.). Class 2 is state industry jobs that pay up to $1.10 an hour (laundry, print shop, chair factory, car tabs, etc.). Class 1 is for private factories from the outside that train and employ prisoners and pay them at least minimum wage to do work that the businesses sell to outside businesses.

About two years earlier, the state started taking 35 percent of all money sent in from friends and family. This included 20 percent for the cost of incarceration, 10 percent for a savings account for when you're released, and 5 percent for a crime victim compensation fund. They also implemented a $3 charge every time you see medical or dental. It makes jobs in prison important to everyone.

Most everything in here is run by prisoners. The guards just let us do our own things, and as long as there is no violence they don't care. It's cool, because once you get your program down you're left alone.

The gym has handball, racquetball, basketball, and pickle ball courts; weight decks inside and outside; and an exercise room with treadmills, stationary bikes, and pull-up and dip bars. Every time you leave the gym you get pat searched.

The yard has a track; softball field; bocce, volleyball, and handball courts; pull-up bars; and picnic tables. The yard is kept up better than most high school ball fields. Every time you leave the yard you get pat searched.

I'm not too sure about all the school classes that they offered here, because I worked the whole time. I did take job readiness and job dynamics, and I know they have GED, Computer Basics, Anger Management, Chemical Dependency, and certified vocational training classes for drafting and welding.

Outside companies bring their businesses inside the prison and pay us minimum wage or more to do the jobs. There are not that many jobs, and the prisoners who have them guard them closely. Before you can even get an interview, you have to know a few people that work there and get them to talk to their boss. After you get the interview, the boss asks all the workers if they have any problems with you. If they don't, you might be hired.

I was lucky, because a few guys that I sat with in the chow hall at Clallam Bay work at one of the companies. They needed someone for an open spot, and when my kitchen time was up they got me working there. I was making $5.85 an hour. Some months I would gross over a thousand dollars. The state also takes 35 percent of all class 1 job pay. Every time you leave work you walk through a metal detector and get pat searched.

This is the first real job I've had in my life. I never worked when I was free. Nobody else goes in your work area, and you don't go in theirs, so many people count on me and job responsibility is very demanding. I also don't want the people that got me the job to look bad, so I really take this seriously and enjoy it.

Not long after I get here a guard doing a tier check sees a prisoner hanging in his cell. The prisoner's cell is on the tier right above me. I heard the guard call an emergency on his radio and then the door slide open. A few minutes later I heard more guards and medical staff showing up, and they say they can't resuscitate him. I hear one of them say, "Deadlock the door and put the crime tape." I get called to a visit, and when I am leaving the unit I see a dead guy lying on the tier without a shirt on.

When I am coming back from my visit a few hours later, I see that the dead guy is still lying on the tier without his shirt on. The guards and all the prisoners are just doing whatever they always do; nobody is talking about it or paying any attention to him. People who live in the cells down the tier from him or going to the showers are stepping over his body.

Right before count, they tell all the prisoners that live in the cells down from him that they need to go to the dayroom to be counted. They say that the local police are coming to investigate and see if a crime happened. During count, many prisoners from above and below the dead guy start yelling from their cells for the guards to get him out of there because he is shitting, pissing, and farting all over himself and it stinks.

After count clears and I leave for dinner I still see the dead guy lying there, but on my way back I see two Monroe police officers taking pictures inside his cell and a couple of nurses standing next to a gurney with a black bag on top. When they call the first nighttime movement, the dead guy is still lying on the floor, but someone has placed a sheet over him. He's been on the tier about six hours. When I come back from the yard later that night he is gone, but I can still smell his waste. I don't remember ever having a conversation with anyone about him lying there.

Just like at my last prison, I don't see my counselor much. Every year he calls me to his office and asks how I'm doing and what I've been up to, and then he tells me I have a yearly review in the next few days. Anytime that I've seen him or asked for something he's been cool and helped me out.

I get into a fight in the gym and I'm cuffed up and walked over to the hole. The hole is in the same building as the units. I am taken to a cell with bars, strip-searched, and given white coveralls, underwear, socks, and slippers.

I am then walked to a tier with about fifteen cells on it and placed in a cell. There is a steel door, bunk, cement desk, toilet, and sink. They come around with books once a day. It is twenty-three-hour-a-day lockdown, like all the other holes. This hole has just been remodeled, so it is clean. There's a lot of yelling and screaming from cell to cell. They don't have an IMU here (Intensive Management Unit), so most of the prisoners in segregation are only there for a short time.

Because of the overcrowding in the prisons, the state is running out of closed custody bed spaces. They begin to send prisoners here that have been in close custody for a while and have not caused any problems. The first year or so it does not make a difference. As more closed custody prisoners show up, more and more problems start to happen. The prison administration warns the population that if this continues there will be changes.

After another stabbing in the yard, the prison is placed on a lockdown for a week. We're then given a new movement schedule—now A & B and C & D will be kept separate. The yard, gym, library, and other programs will now have a rotating schedule. The only time we will see the other units will be at work, at school, and in the visit room.

A week after we get off lockdown, I am in my cell for the 11:00 AM count when about ten guards with a video camera come to my cell and tell me to cuff up. I am escorted to an old closed unit that used to be a hole and placed in a cell with bars.

About forty other prisoners are taken there. They give us a sack lunch with an apple, milk, and a peanut butter and jelly sandwich. After we're done eating, we are told to strip and throw our clothes on the tier. Then they come by and give us orange coveralls and slippers. They say there is a bus waiting outside to take us directly to the Washington State Penitentiary in Walla Walla.

And lot of people start yelling, screaming, and tearing whatever they can in their cells apart, throwing anything they can at the guards, including their shit and piss. It takes about an hour before the guards get their riot gear, helmets, facemasks, body armor, and electric shields and go one by one to all the cells and tell us to cuff up.

Everyone does and one by one they walk us to a room, strip-search us, give us another pair of orange coveralls and slippers, put leg shackles and waist chains on us, and walk us onto the bus.

It is not an easy chain ride. It takes hours to get to Walla Walla, and people are not happy to be leaving. Because of the long ride, we are not chained to each other, so people are moving around from side to side, making the bus rock back and forth, yelling and screaming. As we rounded a few corners, I thought the bus was going to roll. They have a toilet but it won't flush, so people start pissing on the floor. When the bus goes up or down hills the piss rolls up and down the bus. It is the middle of the night when we reach Walla Walla, and we haven't eaten since lunch.

When we get to Walla Walla, we're walked off the bus and escorted to a big room where one by one they take off our chains, take our picture, handcuff us, and escort us through a maze of hallways and into a cell in the hole.

Chapter 4

Washington State Penitentiary

Looking around the cell, I see ants crawling all over the walls. Whoever was here last threw his lunch meal's juice on all the walls. It is very noisy and everything is echoing around the cell because there's nothing in it. There is a bed, desk, toilet, and sink. The front of the cell has a steel door, but the front wall is Plexiglas. There's a bedroll, sack lunch, and Bible on the mattress. They pass out books or do exchanges once a week. I had to wait four days to get any. It takes a long time to clean the juice up, because I only have a roll of toilet paper.

It is hard to sleep because of all the noise and people fishing stuff back and forth all night. They only give you an hour out for recreation every other day here, but on the days we don't get out, we are given showers. When I do get recreation, they handcuff me, take me outside to a walled-off area with six twenty-by-twenty-foot cages, and lock me in one. There are phones in each one and I finally get to call my family and tell them I've been transferred. Every time you leave your cell, your are pat searched.

A day or so after I get here I'm served with my administrative segregation papers, which tell me I'm in the hole for security threat concerns. I go to a hearing after a week and I'm told I will be released to a closed custody population soon.

They have two units for the hole, 1 North and 4 Wing. Each unit is two stories high with four separate tiers, each twenty-six cells long. They have an intensive management unit (IMU) outside the walls of the prison for long-term segregation and death row prisoners.

When I get released from the hole I am handcuffed and walked to the front door of segregation. The guard takes off the cuffs and tells me to go to 7 Wing. I ask where it is and he says, "Over there," and shuts the door. I look around and see a huge wall with guard towers. All the ground is cement and there are two enormous buildings in front of me.

I'm still in my orange coveralls and slippers, and it's so hot the ground is blurry. I walk where he told me and come to the unit door. I have to wait while the guard talks on the phone, looks around, writes something down, asks to see my ID, and then pops the door open. I walk through a metal detector, but there is no guard around to pat search me. I keep walking to another booth, and after a wait he pops that door and then I see a guard in a room with his feet on the desk.

He says, "Name and number."

I tell him, "Wright, 709976."

He looks at a piece of paper and says, "Duck tier, 5 House."

I ask a porter where the duck tier is and he points to a gate. After a wait, the gate slides open and I walk down the tier to my cell. After another wait, the cell bars slide open and I go inside.

The front of the cell is all bars, and I see two guys sitting on the bottom bunks. There are four bunks in the cell, two desks, two bolted-down stools, four small trunks (for our personal property), a toilet, and a sink. There is a bedroll on top of the mattress for me.

I say, "I'm Matt. I have a murder conviction." We talk a little and they tell me who they are and why they are in prison. Then they explain how the prison works.

There are three population units, 6 Wing, 7 Wing, and 8 Wing, and another unit called 5 Wing for protective custody prisoners. All the wings have their own chow halls and movement schedules, except 7 and 8 Wing, which have the same schedule and chow hall. There is a thirty-foot wall around the prison. Everything is cemented except the yard. On one side of the prison are 7 and 8 Wing, and 6 Wing is on the other. The medical floors, 5 Wing, and both holes (4 Wing and 1 North) are in between. In front of the units are the chow halls, kitchen, clothing room, property room, gym, and on top of them the law and regular library, band room, and some school classrooms. There is a hobby shop in front of 6 Wing and the yard next to it.

The duck tier eats last. I still have on my bright orange coveralls and slippers when they called chow. It is very dangerous not to have shoes on in prison and worse if you have slippers. When I walk into the chow hall, I see that they have a catwalk and booth above it with a guard holding a shotgun. There are two lines waiting to get their trays with a metal rail dividing them. The blacks and Mexicans go to the left and the whites and Indians go to the right. They have white workers to one side and black workers on the other side passing out trays.

As I'm getting my tray, one of my buddies comes up and points me to his table. Everything is aged, raced, and cliqued off. He tells me he will bring a kite to breakfast for me. I don't know what he's talking about, and before I can ask the guard comes by and tells him to tray up. You're allowed only twenty minutes to eat whether you're done or not.

They randomly pat search people as they leave the chow hall. I walk back to the unit and after the long waits, cell in. This unit has no movement that night, so I can't leave my cell until breakfast.

The porter brings me a chain bag and there's only a three-inch toothbrush, toothpaste, and a bar of soap. My cellies tell me that 7 Wing is for any prisoners working full time and who want to live around other prisoners that work. It's supposed to be a lot quieter and less stressful.

The protective custody unit has its own chow hall and no one leaves except in the morning, when the rest of the population is on unit lockdown. They get a choice of yard, gym, or law or regular libraries. They have their callouts then. From afternoon and evening, 6, 7, and 8 Wings rotate their movements and have a choice of yard, gym, or libraries.

We are in our cell here about twenty hours a day. You get out for meals and afternoon or evening movements only. Showers are run in the morning. When they call your tier for showers, you put your sign out and they let you out. In 7 Wing there are three shower stalls per tier. They tell me that I will stay on the duck tier until I get a kite from a cell where all the prisoners have signed it saying I can move in. Every Tuesday I will be called for a review, and if have a kite I give it to them then.

The next afternoon I go to the clothing room and get my state-issue clothing. There's a cage outside the clothing room that we're locked in until everyone there is finished. I also go to the yard. It is very big; there is a track, two softball fields, three handball courts, two basketball courts, pull-up bars, and a row of phones against the wall. Everyone is pat searched by a row of guards to and from the yard.

During yard, my buddy tells me to look at the handball courts. About a minute later, I see a white guy start to punch another white guy. The yard is silent. I hear this loud cocking sound and over the speaker system, "Everybody lay down." The four towers that circle the yard all have a guard on their catwalks with shotguns pointing at the two guys fighting. They say over the speaker, "Last warning before we shoot," and the two guys stop and lay down. About ten guards then run on the yard, handcuff them and place these black masks over their heads, and walked them out of the yard. The black masks are to keep them from spitting on the guards. Everybody gets back up and starts laughing and playing as they were.

After yard, a porter brings me a kite from a friend that's over in 6 Wing, so when I go to the review I give them that one instead of turning in the kite from my buddy in 8 Wing. I haven't seen my buddy in 6 Wing for a few years and I trust him and would like to catch up. At the review they ask me if I have any enemies or concerns. I say no. They tell me to stand and take off my shirt and turn around. They then bring out a camera and take pictures of my body. They tell me they will move me to 6 Wing but into a different cell until the unit sergeant there can talk with me and see if he wants me in the cell I asked for. They also have me sign a form saying I know they have the right to shoot me if I refuse an order to stop an attack on another person.

The next afternoon I get escorted to 6 Wing. You have to go through a metal detector after you walk in and then go down a hallway through two doors, past the dayroom, and into the unit. There are two sides to the unit, which is three tiers high and fifteen cells long. All cells have four bunks.

I am on the bottom tier and it is filthy. They do not give you garbage cans for the cells and you don't leave the cells much so garbage is thrown out the cell bars. I've never seen it like this before. It is deafeningly loud; there's all this shouting from cell to cell and in the cells. You can hear the dominos slapping down on the desks and garbage keeps crashing down on the floor. The bottom floor is covered with trash and burning cigarette butts. The cigarette butts sometimes light the other garbage on the floor on fire, and there's always this burnt paper and plastic smell in the air.

I go to my cell and there are two guys in there. I tell them who I am and find out who they are and make my bed up. The two guys are not talking to each other, so I just lie on my bed and read a magazine one of them had. They have no personal stuff of their own.

At dinner my buddy tells me I will be moving into his cell after lunch tomorrow. It is on the second tier thankfully. I'm sitting at his table in the chow hall. Three of the four people who sit at the table were tablemates at Clallam Bay.

They have a dayroom down the hall from the unit that is opened during yard and every other night when we don't have yard. Each side of the unit takes turns using the dayroom for one hour at a time. They have phones, a pool table, and card tables in there.

Because we are in a four-man cell and locked down most of the time, if you are all in you bunks, it is common courtesy not to look at the other bunks in the cell or sleep facing the wall.

Besides counts, the guards do not do regular tier checks. When they do come on the tier, no matter what time it is, people always yell out "one time," meaning a guard is on the tier. That night when my cellie rolls over and faces the wall to sleep, the other cellie puts a few bars of soap into a couple of pairs of socks and starts beating the other guy up.

I am sitting up on my bunk watching him beat him and I hear him yelling, "I ain't living with no AIDS victim." I grab my blanket as fast as I can and covered my body. I don't know what's going on, but I'm not getting any blood on me. The guy falls out of his bed and onto the floor and is not moving and bleeding badly. After a while, the guy stops beating him up.

I tell him he should get the dude's face over the toilet and that I'm not cleaning any blood up. He says when the dude gets up he will clean up his own blood. It is a bloody mess. It gets cleaned up, but I can't wait to move.

I move and it is a lot better being around people I can trust. They have all their own property, so at least I can watch TV until my property shows up. You're allowed only one TV per cell, and with four people living around each other in a small cell, it can get tense. The guy I used to live with that got beat up went to the guards a few days later and said he fell out of the bed and needed medical help. I haven't seen him since.

All cells are searched once a month by a team of guards. The difference with cell searches here is that the team comes storming down the tier in the middle of the night like a SWAT team. They make everyone freeze and then strip us one by one and escort us to the dayroom and search the cell.

All day and all night there is a rumbling noise. It calms down at night, but the night brings other noises. Every night I hear people fighting, talking, arguing, moaning, and grunting, and tattoo guns are always rattling and buzzing. People sleep when people sleep.

I like where I live, but all my cellies do is shoot dope and hustle up other prisoners' prescription pills. They have only one needle and they do not clean it. They get all angry if the dope doesn't come in or if the dope guy is late and all happy when they have it in their hands. After they shoot their dope they laugh, sweat, kick back and nod off, throw up, and shoot more, every chance they get. Mood swings are common in the cells.

They run showers here tier by tier and everyone gets ten minutes. Since they run showers only once a day, everyone goes and it gets crowded. The shower room is about thirty feet by thirty feet with fifteen showerheads over three walls and a Plexiglas booth with a guard in it on the other. In the shower room, we stand shoulder to shoulder waiting to get some water. It is very crowded and dangerous because there are usually more than fifty prisoners trying to use the few showerheads. Each race has its own showerheads and they do not use any others. We get in line behind a showerhead, get wet as fast as possible, and get in the back of the line. While waiting at the back of the line, we soap and shampoo up. When we get back to a showerhead, we rinse off and then go to a bench in the middle the room to dry off.

My second time in the showers I am getting wet when I notice how quiet it is. I look around and see a guy holding his neck with blood running through his fingers and down his body. There's always so much water that it cannot drain fast enough. I see the water is turning pink and it is getting closer to me. I put on my underwear and walk back to my cell wet.

I write a kite to the counselor to call me out, and a week later I see him and ask why I'm in closed custody when I have medium points. He looks on the computer and says he does not know and he will get back to me. He does not say anything about work or school. They don't care about that here.

I get called to the property room two months after I get here and issued my personal property. My TV goes into storage, because my cellie already has one. I have been wearing state-issue clothing all the hot summer long. I need more comfortable clothes. There is a cage in front of the property room where we are locked in while we wait for everyone to get their property.

The guard comes to your cell and asks for your ID to check it against any mail you might have before he will give it to you. They pass it around after the 4:00 PM count. You can have most newspapers, magazines, and catalogs sent to you by your family or purchased off your account. Letters, pictures, and drawings are allowed, but everything has to have you name and number written on the back.

I do not know anything about school, chapel, visit room, gym, or anything other than the chow hall and yard. They're the only places I went before I left.

About four months after I get here, the counselor calls me back to his office and tells me I will be leaving in the morning for the medium custody building. That night I am given some boxes and told to bring my stuff to the dayroom. It is inventoried and put on a cart.

The next morning a guard comes to my cell and walks me to the receiving unit and I'm strip-searched, given orange coveralls, leg shackled, waist chained, and walked outside into a little bus that holds about ten prisoners. We drive outside the walls and about two minutes later through the gates of the medium custody prison.

Chapter 5

Washington State Penitentiary Medium Security Unit

After going through the gates, we stop and are told to get off the bus. We are escorted to the receiving unit, and one by one our chains are removed and we have our pictures taken for new IDs. Next we are escorted to a unit called Baker. The prison looks very nice and clean. It's all landscaped with flower gardens and cement pathways through kept grass. It doesn't feel threatening or imposing.

You have to go through two sliding doors to get in. To your left is a unit office and supply room, and there is a round guard booth in the middle of a rotunda with three pods surrounding it that have Plexiglas fronts. We go to the office and check in, then to the booth to show our IDs and get a cell key and assignment. Baker unit has one pod just for new prisoners (ducks). The cells have a steel door, two bunks, a moveable wood desk and chair, a toilet, and a sink.

They run ten-minute hourly movements from 8:00 AM to 8:00 PM except counts (11:00 AM and 4:00 PM), when you can leave your cell, go to the dayroom, shower, phone, chapel, Coke shack, or recreation. Besides chow and callouts, movements are the only time you can leave your cells. Once you go somewhere, you have to wait for the next movement to leave. We have a key to our cells so we can let ourselves in whenever we want. Everyone is locked in his cell from 9:00 PM to 6:00 AM.

The pods are three tiers high and eleven two-man cells long. There is a dayroom in the front of the first tier that is divided by a spiral staircase. There are three tables on each side of the stairs and three phones on one wall. In the middle of the first tier there is a large open space that has a personal laundry room and three shower stalls.

After all the other pods and units have eaten, they call the duck pod for chow. I am still in my orange coverall's and slippers. The chow hall is mostly empty, so I eat and walk back to my pod. They randomly pat search everyone to and from chow. After lunch, I am told to walk behind the unit to a building that has a clothing room, as well as a law and regular library. I go to the clothing room and receive my state clothing.

In this prison, there are three units, Adams, Baker, and Rainer, for more secure prisoners and one unit, Blue Mountain (BMU), for less secure prisoners. Where you go depends on your infraction record and offense, but everyone here is medium custody.

The prison has three units in a row, with the building for the clothing room and law and regular library behind it. In front of them, you have the main entrance to the prison to the right and a line of buildings on the left. In front of the last unit is a building for the chapel. Next to it is a long, big building with the medical floor, receiving area, and administration offices, and a visiting room on the second floor above them. Next to that building is a building with the property room and Coke shack, then the unit called Blue Mountain (BMU). Next to BMU is the Recreation Department, with the gym, band room, hobby shop, and gym showers. In front of the gym but separated by the yard is the Correctional Industries Department.

The prison is surrounded by guard towers and two fences with razor wire wrapped around the top and filled in between them.

Recreation is set up differently than in other places. They have the yard with a track, softball field, and pull-up bars, an outside weight deck, a patio (with picnic tables), and three handball courts. However, there's a building that is surrounded by the yard, outside weight deck and handball courts. The building has a gym with a basketball and pickle ball court, exercise machines, shower room, weight room, hobby shop, and band room. When you're at recreation you can go between the yard and gym whenever you want.

While we're in the duck pod we cannot have personal property. We have to go through an orientation with a counselor and someone from the school floor. The counselor tells us that everyone who does not have a program is to check in at their unit duty office by 7:30 AM to see if the guards have any work that the unit needs done. If they do, you have to work at least thirty minutes and you do not get paid for this work.

The counselor lets us know that nothing will be tolerated here. They have a bus ready for anyone at all times to take them back inside the walls if they misbehave. We will be in the duck pod until orientation is over, and we get a unit review and they decide where we are best fit to live. If possible, we should have a kite with a cell we would like to go to. We can move from cell to cell whenever we want, but we're not allowed to live with other races without a unit review, and our cellies cannot be ten years older or ten years younger than us.

The school department comes and tells us they have GED, Computer, Writing, Anger Management, Chemical Dependency, Achieving Your Potential, Critical Thinking, and Victim Awareness classes. They have two certified courses for custodial services and automotive repair and painting. They tell us that anyone with more than ten years to serve can enroll only in GED, self-help groups, and custodial services. The school floor is in the basement of BMU.

They have a booth in the outside corner of BMU that they call the Coke shack. You go to the window with a form filled out with what you want and hand the staff your ID. It gets scanned, the money is removed from your account, and you go to the next window for your purchases. They sell cooked pizzas, burritos, pretzels, tater tots, chicken, cinnamon rolls, and different candies and sodas.

When I go to my unit review I'm told I have to live in the pods and will not be allowed to move to BMU while I am here. I tell them I have a buddy in Adams unit whose cellie is leaving soon. They put me in his pod in a cell by myself and tell me I will have a couple of weeks to find a cellie. Then they tell me to take off my shirt to take pictures of any scars or tattoos.

The same day I move to Adams unit I get called to the property room and issued my personal property. It is nice having a few days alone to set my cell up and relax.

I start sitting with my buddy, whom I also sat with at Clallam Bay. The chow hall is raced off and cliqued off like everywhere else, but this chow hall feels more laid back. A couple of weeks later I move into my friend's cell.

I get my first visit after eight months. The visiting room is nice. We are so far away from things that only a few people are visiting. They have vending machines and microwaves. The place is clean and the guards don't bother us. I get pat searched on the way in and out. This is the first visiting room I've been to where I haven't been strip-searched after a visit. It takes my family seven hours to drive one way. Visiting is Friday through Monday, 10:00 AM to 8:00 PM.

We have all this freedom here and the prison is really clean and nice, but it is next to closed custody and everyone knows that at any second we could get run back inside. There is not much stuff going on here, some fights and tattooing, but mostly people just stay within their cliques and do their own thing. The politics and attitudes are the same as in closed custody.

Since you are required to have a certificate to get a porter job, I sign up for the custodial class and a few months later I get a custodial certificate. I start working as a pod porter. My paychecks are about $25 a month.

The chapel, hobby shop, and band room are open whenever recreation is. The chapel has different religious services and programs throughout the week.

The barbershop is in a little room in the Rainier unit rotunda, and it has all the tools a barbershop needs. When you leave the barbershop your hair has to be at least a quarter of an inch long.

The guards come around after the 4:00 PM count and slide any mail you have under your door. To get magazines, newspapers, and catalogs they will call you down to the unit office and give them to you. You can purchase most newspapers, magazines, and catalogs using your account or have your family purchases them for you. They also can send letters, pictures, and drawings as long as they have your name and number on the back.

They post a callout sheet on the pod bulletin board daily for the next day's callouts. If you miss an appointment, you can be infracted.

I don't go to dental and medical that often, but I do see the dentist here and have the best dental appointment of my life. He checks all over my face and neck for bumps and every spot in my mouth. I also get my first teeth cleaning in years.

When I first got here, I went to the counselor and asked if I could have a hardship transfer back to WSR because my mom has cancer. He said I had to do one year infraction free before he would consider it.

About five months later I go back to the counselor with a doctor's note saying my mom is sick and can't drive and ask for a hardship transfer back to WSR. He says, "No, you need to wait at least a year." I do get the trailer forms, and about a month later I am approved for trailer visits. Walla Walla is so far for my family that I haven't gotten one.

I'm not doing anything special here. I'm working as a porter and working out daily. The prison is the nicest that I have been too. If it was closer to home I would not want to leave. However, just because the prison is nice and relaxed does not mean that things aren't as serious and as dangerous as anywhere else. Because of the extra freedom, most of the fear and violence happens behind closed doors, but you do see and hear of stuff.

A skinhead shot caller got transferred from closed custody to here. When he gets to chow hall he sees a very light-skinned mulatto sitting there. He says, "Why is this half-breed sitting here?" One of the skin heads says, "He invited him," and nods at another skinhead. The shot caller tells the mulatto dude to go somewhere else and he lets the other skinheads know how fucked up that he thinks they are. He tells the guy who invited him to meet him at the gym next movement.

When the dude gets to the gym they go into the bathroom and the shot caller hands him a tattoo gun. He tells him that if he covers his tattoos he can stay on mainline but that he would not be welcome with the skinheads anymore. The skinhead has a tattoo of a swastika on his stomach and white pride down the backs of his arms. He doesn't have much of a choice, because if he tries to fight a shot caller he will be a target in any prison he goes to. But if he covers up his tattoos he will be seen as a weak person and most prisoners will shun him or make him a mission boy to stay in population. A couple of days later I see him sitting at the ding table with a solid black bar of ink down the backs of his arms.

About a month after I see the counselor asking for a transfer I get called down to the counselor's office and meet my new counselor. The old counselor moved to another prison. She tells me that the policy has changed for first degree murder and I'm allowed to have minimum custody. I asked why and was told that they don't have any more bed spaces for long-term medium prisoners and they want to send the ones that don't have problems to minimum custody to make room.

I tell her about my family's medical problems and ask if I can have a hardship transfer to Twin Rivers. She schedules me for a transfer review the next week. When I go to the review they tell me that someone has placed a "separatee" on me at Twin Rivers (see glossary), and until it's removed or he transfers I can't go there. They then request a transfer to McNeil Island for me.

Six weeks later I get my review paperwork back saying that McNeil Island will not accept first-degree murder charges. I see my counselor and she schedules me for another review. She tells me they will transfer me to McNeil Island on a hardship and recommend that when the guy with the separatee against me leaves Twin Rivers I will be transferred there.

Twin Rivers is a medium and minimum custody prison that is in the same complex as WSR. It takes some long-term prisoners but mostly short term. I don't ask for WSR, because it is a prison for closed and medium custody prisoners only and I'm getting promoted to minimum. McNeil Island is a minimum custody prison that is evenly split between short- and long-term prisoners.

I've been in or around closed custody facilities for ten years. I'm around the same people doing the same thing every day. I hate it, but it's what I know. I sleep well every night, knowing if something happens and I go somewhere, I will know someone. I don't know anything about minimum custody and I will have to start over. I'm not excited, but thankfully I will be transferring.

A month later I get called to the booth and told to grab some boxes, pack what I will need for my chain boxes, and box the rest of my stuff and bring it to the property room for shipping to McNeil Island.

About four in the morning the next day, I am woken up and told to go to the dayroom. I am then escorted to a room where I'm strip-searched, given a pair of orange coveralls and slippers, have my legs shackled and waist chains placed on me, and walked outside to the chain bus. After a little wait, we drive through two gates and head to the R-units.

Chapter 6

McNeil Island Corrections Center

It's Wednesday when I leave MSU and go to the R-units. The chain bus to McNeil Island is on Thursday. We get off the bus and walk into the receiving unit, take off our chains, eat our sack lunch, and walk over to R-4.

They have me sleeping on the floor of a cell this time. I eat dinner and listen to the radio until the porter brings me my chain bag. Since I just got here, I don't put anything in it. I go to sleep and at 5:00 AM I get woken up and told to go to the dayroom. I am escorted to receiving, am chained up, eat a sack lunch, get on the bus, wait for the guards' break, and leave for McNeil Island.

About half an hour later, the bus stops and through the front window I see that we're getting on a barge. We're locked in a bus with our bodies chained up and they're taking us across the Puget Sound to McNeil Island. The bus is slowly rocking back and forth as we are crossing. When get to the other side and off the barge it's about a two-minute drive to the gates of the prison.

We drive through two gates and stop at an angle on a hill, where we're told to get off the bus. We walk into a building that looks like its fifty years old. They unchain us and give us a sack lunch.

After we eat, one by one we go into a room where a lady asks us if we are gang members or have any enemies here. She then has us take off our shirts to photograph any tattoos. After that we walk one by one down the hallway to the clothing room and get our state-issue clothing. Then we go to the property room, which is the next room over, and they issue us our chain boxes and bags.

My chain boxes are not there. I am upset that I have to wait for next week's chain to get any personal stuff, and I don't know how long it will take to ship the rest of my property, but having your stuff go someplace else and them not finding it happens a lot. The guard gives us our units and cell assignments, then points the way and we walk to our units.

The prison is surrounded by guard towers and two fences with coils of razor wire on top of them and between them. The prison is built on a hill overlooking Puget Sound. There are five population units and one hole/intensive management unit (IMU). Each unit has an upper and lower section, each two rectangular tiers high and twenty-five cells long. The units are rectangular, with the dayroom in the middle of the tiers. On each end of the tiers are restrooms and showers. In the middle of the front wall is the guard's desk, personal laundry room, ice room, and an old counselor's office that now has four bunks and is used for new prisoners.

The cells do not have toilets or sinks. They have two bunks, two steel desks, two lockers, and two moveable chairs. We have wooden doors and keys to our cells. I hate community bathrooms. All cells are searched once a month by two guards.

At the top of the hill are the five units, A, B, C, D, E, and the hole/IMU. In front of them is a huge building that has the hobby shop, chapel, regular and law library, administration offices, chow hall, and band room. On the second floor is the school department and on the third floor is the medical department. At the back corner of the building is a staircase that leads to a tunnel that goes to property and clothing rooms. Next to the building is another building with the kitchen and another chow hall. Next to them is the gym.

Down the hill a little ways is the work compound, which has the state laundry, steam plant, correctional industries, trailers, bike shop (used to repair children's bikes that are donated and then given back to charities), welding shop, and a building with vocational programs and custodial services. At the bottom of the hill is the yard.

The gym has a basketball court, weight room, and two full racquetball courts. You are pat searched whenever you leave the gym.

The yard is very large. It has a track, softball field, weight deck, pull-up bars, and basketball and handball courts. The yard is almost water level and has a nice view of the sound. You have to go through a metal detector and get pat searched entering and leaving the yard.

We can leave our cells for the bathroom anytime we need to and for the dayroom when it's opened. The dayroom is open from 6:00 AM to 11:00 PM, except count time. Unless you have a work assignment, you are in your cells for counts at 4:00 PM, 9:00 PM, and from 11:00 PM to 6:00 AM.

They have movements to leave the units every hour. You can go to the yard, gym, library, law library, hobby shop, band room, callouts, and the chapel. The yard and gym are open for everyone in the morning and on a rotating schedule for the units in the afternoon and evening. Once you go somewhere you are stuck until the next movement.

Callouts are posted on the unit bulletin board every night for the next day. If you miss an appointment you can be infracted.

They put me in the four-man duck room until a cell opens up. You get the first cell that opens up no matter what race lives there. Once you get a cell it is your cell until you leave. They do not do courtesy cell moves here. I go to the unit sergeant's office and talk with her about my forty-year sentence. This will not be the last prison I go to, I tell her, and it could be hard on me in the future if I were to live with a different race. I tell her I cannot allow myself to be put in a position that might cause grief for me in the future regardless of the consequences now.

She tells me that this is a minimum custody prison that is preparing prisoners for re-entry to life outside of the prison, and that means being able to get along with all kinds of people. She has to give me this speech, even though she won't live by it. She does not want any more problems in the unit than there already are—or any more paperwork. A few days later I get moved into a cell with a white guy.

I live in prison. I'm not getting out next week or next year; this is my home. When you get a cell, it becomes your home. You have to be comfortable where you live and with whom you live. You have to be able to trust your cellie enough to leave your stuff alone with him and protect it when you're not home. I will not live in a situation where I know I will not be comfortable or feel safe.

My cellie is almost fifty years old, with long gray hair and a beard to his waist. He does not have any personal property, and all his state clothes are run down and worn out. He tells me he has been in prison three times over the last twenty years, and now he's doing a twenty-five-year sentence. He tells me he's a dope fiend and all he wants to do is shoot dope and asks if that will be a problem. I tell him I don't care what he does as long as he respects my stuff and rides his own beefs.

He has just won a lawsuit against the state for $9,000. He has a couple of guys stop by the cell a few times a day and he buys these little papers of heroin from them. He cooks his dope, shoots it, and lies in his bed. He doesn't buy any personal property or store and barely goes to the chow hall or showers. He just shoots his dope and junkies out.

A gram of heroin cost about $80 on the street; in here you pay $200. With a gram of dope in here you can make four $100 sacks for sale, and if you want you can sell half to pay for the dope and shoot the other half. He buys these little papers for one hundred dollars, two or three times a day. I ask him why he doesn't buy grams and he tells me they won't sell him grams.

Everyone around here knows he's a dope fiend. They will not cut a dope fiend any breaks, because they know he will buy anything to get high. He might complain and bicker but he will always take it because he has to have it. I lived with him for six months and he did not stop shooting dope until he ran out of money. (He ran out about four months after I moved in.)

I heard that after I transferred he got beat up badly over a debt. I don't know if it's true, but I know who he was dealing with and this guy wouldn't forget a ten-cent debt.

The chow hall is raced off and cliqued off, just like everywhere else. I didn't think I would know anyone when I was coming here, but I am running into people I know. I start sitting with someone I sat with at WSR.

There are not that many Mexicans in this prison, so they have only one table in the chow hall. If all of them show up for chow or the ones that get their first don't eat fast enough, there's not enough room for them all to sit.

There is not any room at his table for this Mexican to sit, so he puts his tray down on the table next to his and slowly goes to get some water and wait for a spot to open. A black guy walks up to him and he tells him he needs to move his tray. The next thing I see is the two dudes fighting, and then the Mexican and black tables all start fighting each other.

This happened on my second day here, and I see that some things are always the same: no matter where you go or what custody level you get, you still have to have your space. Right or wrong, if you feel that someone is crowding your space you have to do something, because if you don't they might start crowding your space until you don't have any space left.

My buddy got me working with him as a porter in the visiting room. It's a good job, because I only have to go down to the visit room for about an hour a night. We just get things cleaned up and ready for the next day's visits. It pays about $20 a month.

It takes two weeks to get my chain boxes, because they got sent to the wrong prison. About a week later, I get the rest of my personal property. To go to the property room you have to wait for your name to get on the callout sheet, then go to the hallway in the main building leading to the property room, wait for movement to close, have a guard check our names against the callout list, and then walk down as a group to the property room. We cannot leave until everyone we came with is finished.

This prison has the best schooling I've been around. They have certified vocational courses for dry walling, plumbing, custodial services, welding, and house framing. They have school classes for computers, writing, GED, and more. There are self-help groups for anger management, chemical dependency, job readiness, victim awareness, parenting, and long-distance dads.

The politics and attitudes are the same as in other prisons, but they're not as strictly followed here. I see many people living with other races whereas at other prisons they would have problems.

The guards will come around to your cell and pass out mail during tier checks in the afternoon or after the 4:00 PM count. You can purchase most magazines, newspapers, catalogs, and books using your account or have your family purchase them for you. They can also send letters, pictures, and drawings.

The barbershop is across from the hobby shop. You can walk down during movements and wait for an open chair. The barbershop has most tools for cutting hair.

I get a visit about a week after I get here. It is really comfortable in the visit, which has a pro-family environment. They have vending machine, microwaves, and a crafts section for kids. They give out sack lunches during lunchtime and the guards go out of their way to be friendly. Visiting is four days a week from 9:30 AM to 2:30 PM. Everyone is pat searched on the way in and strip-searched on the way out.

The bad part of the visit room is that our loved ones have to take a ferry to the prison. Our visitors have to be at Western State Hospital by either 8:00 AM or 9:00 AM to check in and get on a state bus. Those are the only two times they can come to the visit room. The bus drives to a prison dock, where our families get on a ferry for a twenty-minute ride. They dock at the prison and then have to walk half a mile to the visit room. It's very hard on the elderly and children. There are only three ferries that leave the visit room, at 12:30 PM, 1:30 PM, and 2:30 PM. The process of them getting in takes an hour and a half.

The law and regular library, hobby shop, band room, and chapel are open for everyone most movements. The chapel has different groups and services throughout the week.

The landscaping is nice around the prison and the units are clean and in good shape. They have a list in the unit that you can sign to get your cell painted whenever you want. I've never seen that happen in prison before.

The store has a bigger selection than in the other prisons. It's more of the same stuff, except they have microwaves in all the units' dayrooms, so they sell microwave popcorn, muffins, and prepared stews.

The dayroom is big. They have about twenty-five four-man tables and four rows of five phones along the edges. They have two microwaves, an ice room, and a personal laundry that you can use whenever the dayroom is open.

I see my counselor and ask if I can get the trailer forms so I can send them out to my family. He says since I just had the form sent at MSU he would just give me a hearing. I was approved and got one trailer before I was transferred. I tell him about a seperatee that I knew nothing about and say that if I get to Twin Rivers I will not cause any problems. I ask if I can have a hardship transfer to Twin Rivers and show him my family's doctor's notes. He says he will look into it.

The trailers are old but nice. Our loved ones drive to the dock and take the ferry across, then get picked up at the dock and driven into the prison trailer compound. At my trailer, the guard helps my family carry their food and clothing up to the trailer. They have everything in them that WSR has, but the trailers also have a VCR. We can even check out movies and watch them.

About eight months after I get here, I am called to the guard's desk and told to grab some boxes and pack out for a transfer to Twin Rivers. I make up my two chain boxes and pack the rest up and bring it to the desk. The next morning at about nine, I am called to the property room to fill out the forms to mail my stuff and walk down the hall to get chained up.

This prison provides a good experience for visitors and has some very good school classes and programs. One program, called Long Distance Dads, goes out of the way to help you build and maintain bonds with your children. A few times a year they will close the yard and let you bring your kids out to ride bikes, play softball, walk around the track, and have a picnic with them.

This prison has more drugs than I've seen at other prisons, but there's not much violence. I saw only a few fights and fresh tattoos when I was there. There are so many work opportunities, classes, and programs that everyone is in his own world, and because of that nobody wants to bother with anybody. They also have a big library full of good current books. You would never believe it was a prison library if you walked into it. The noise level in the units gets bad in the evening, but at night it's okay. If you are motivated, you can learn a lot in this prison.

Chapter 7

Twin Rivers Corrections Center

When we get to the R-units, we get off the bus and are taken to receiving, where we are unchained and given a sack lunch. After getting our coveralls and shoes, we walk over to R-4, where we get our cell assignments. It is a Thursday when I get here, and the chain to Twin Rivers is not until Monday. Nothing has changed here.

The chain ride from the receiving units to Twin Rivers is an hour or so. When we get to Twin Rivers, we drive through two gates and stop outside receiving. We're taken inside and wait on a bench to have our chains removed. We then wait our turn and take a picture for new IDs, then receive our state clothing and cell assignments.

In my unit, there is a rotunda with a guard booth, a laundry room for personal clothes, and a sergeant's and custody unit supervisor's (CUS) office. There are three wings in front of the guard's booth, all with Plexiglas window fronts. The wings are two tiers high and twenty-one two-man cells long. There is a dayroom at the end of each tier. The dayrooms have two phones, card tables, and three shower stalls.

I go to the booth and show my ID and I'm given a chain packet, cell key, and assignment. They have about eight single cells per wing, and I'm going to sleep on the floor of one and until a cell opens up. I get a cell three days later.

The cells have two bunks, a desk, two moveable chairs, a toilet, and a sink. They also have big windows with bars in front of them. The windows can be opened. We have keys to our cells, and we can go in and out whenever we want, but we can only leave the unit for callouts and movements. You can move cells if you want to move, but once you do, you are in that cell for six months. All cells are searched once a month by two guards.

They have movements every hour from 7:30 AM to 7:50 PM. During movement, you can go to the yard or gym. You have to check out passes from the booth if you want to go to the law library, regular library, or chapel. The gym is open whenever movement is, and the yard is open until it gets dark. Everyone is locked down from 9:00 PM to 6:00 AM.

When I read the chain packet, I see that they have a lot of school classes and self-help programs. I go to an orientation the day after I get here and I'm told about the classes and programs. They tell me this is a prison and a treatment facility. They have one unit here where sex offenders can volunteer and receive sex offender treatment. I'm told that anyone who interferes with the treatment of an offender will be placed in the hole and transferred to another facility.

The chow hall is very relaxed. It is raced and cliqued off, like everywhere else, but I have not seen any fights over the seats. I sit with someone I used to sit with at Clallam Bay. A & B and C & D units have their own chow halls. They randomly pat search everyone leaving the chow hall.

The day I moved from the floor to a cell, I get called to the property room and issued my two chain boxes. The next week I get the rest of my personal property. The property room has an open callout for anyone during the week from 12:15 PM to 12:30 PM.

This prison is built in an egg shape. There are four units. A unit is for the sex offender treatment prisoners, B unit is for medium custody prisoners, while C and D are for the minimum custody prisoners. In front of the four units are the sex offender treatment program, visiting room, administration offices, medical, two chow halls, property, clothing room, library, maintenance department, school floor, a building with the chapel, barbershop, law library, gym, hobby shop, and yard.

The gym has a weight deck; basketball, handball, and pickle ball courts; exercise machines; punching bag; and an outside fenced-in cement yard with a tennis court and handball courts.

The yard has a track, softball field, pull-up bars, bocce court, and tables. You can bring books and magazines to the yard.

You don't get pat searched leaving the gym or yard, but there are guards standing on the breezeway leading to and from them who randomly pat search prisoners.

I see my counselor when I first get here and get the forms my family needs for trailer visits. About a month later, I get a trailer review and approved. The counselor, custody unit supervisor, and sergeant all have an open-door policy when they are in.

Twin Rivers does not have a hole or trailers. The Washington State Reformatory (WSR) is next door and anyone going to the trailers or the hole is transported there. For the transporting, you go to the receiving unit, where you are strip-searched, given the orange coveralls and slippers, and chained at the leg and waist. You are then put into a van and driven to WSR. When you get there you are unchained, strip-searched, and taken to the hole or dressed and walked to your trailer visit.

The guards do mail call before the 4:00 PM count in the dayroom. They call it and everyone goes to the dayroom to see if they have anything. You can purchase most newspapers, magazines, catalogs, and books on your account or you can have your family order them for you. You can have letters, pictures, and drawings sent in.

The visit room is clean and quiet. It is big, with a Plexiglas wall dividing it in half, cutting down the noise. They have vending machines and microwaves. I have never had any problems with the visit room. It is open four days a week from 12:30 PM to 8:30 PM.

When I moved off the floor, they put me in a cell with a guy who had about fifteen years left. We got along okay and lived together for ten months. He was married. His wife didn't work, so she came to visit him every visit day, start to finish. When they weren't visiting he was on the phone with her all day.

He went to a visitor one day and later that night two guards came to our cell and handed me his gold chain and wedding ring. They tell me he signed a waiver for his property because he was placed on shit watch.

The property waiver is for when you are leaving your cell for various reasons, such as trailer, medical, and court. You can sign a property waiver saying the state is not responsible for any lost or damaged property and they will leave your property in the cell until you get back.

Shit watch is when the prison thinks you swallowed contraband or put contraband up your butt. They put you in coveralls that lock around the neck, wrists, and ankles. Then they put you in a room on the medical floor with nothing in it but a mattress and surveillance camera. To get out of the room you have to give three good full shits in a bucket. The guard then checks the shit for any contraband, and if it's clean you go back to population. If they find something you go to the hole for whatever punishment they're giving you.

Three days later the guards come to my cell, cuff me up, and tell me they need me to give a urine sample. Then they walk me to receiving, tell me to fill out some forms, strip-search me, and watch me pee in a cup. I then walk back to my unit and wait in the dayroom as two guards search my cell and check our store items against our store receipts and personal property against our property matrix. They then pack up all his property and tell me he's gone to the hole.

A few days after that I get a letter in the mail from his wife saying that he's doing okay, but they found two grams of cocaine in his shit. He has told her to tell me, "Phone calls cost money. I'll see you around."

A few weeks after that I get a letter from her. The Department of Corrections sent her a letter saying she would not be allowed to visit her husband again as long as he was under the custody of the Washington State Department of Corrections.

The biggest difference between closed custody and minimum custody is that in minimum, programs are not compulsory. The people there *want* to be there. When I go to the school floor to find out more about the classes offered I see people in classrooms working and helping each other instead of laughing and doing whatever they can to disrupt things and get out of class.

They have some very good classes and programs. The school offers courses in computer repair, multimedia, information technology, writing, GED, and math. There are self-help classes and groups such as Anger Management, Chemical Dependency, Victim Awareness, Alternatives to Violence, Parenting, Alcoholics Anonymous, and Narcotics Anonymous. You have to clear a metal detector and pat search every time you leave the school floor.

They also have a group for veterans and an organization called Community Aid Coalition (CAC). The CAC is a nonprofit organization that does volunteer work like fundraisers and craft making to sell at auctions. All the money they make is donated to charity.

I get a porter job in the unit a few weeks after I get here. The most you can make at any job is $52 a month.

If you want to go to medical, you sign up on an appointment sheet that medical posts. It takes about a week to see anyone. I have not had any serious medical or dental needs, but for the little stuff that comes up I have not had a problem getting anything done. You are pat searched every time you leave the medical floor.

I have seen a fight or two and some tattooing, but this prison is not violent. There's a large population of homosexuals. In other prisons, they might wear makeup or act flamboyantly, but the sexual stuff is always behind closed doors. Here it is a very sexual environment. You see couples walking around holding hands, kissing behind doors or in blind spots. They perform sexual acts under tables and going in and out of cells. It is very different for me, but as long as I do my own thing I am not bothered.

They have a lot of chapel programs and groups at different times during the week for anyone to attend. The first Sunday of every month, they have a religious service in the visiting room that your families can attend with you.

There is a list outside the barbershop where you can sign up and have your hair cut whenever there's an opening. The barbershop has most tools needed to cut hair.

They post the next day's callouts on every wing's bulletin board nightly. It seems as if every time I walk by the wing bulletin boards, I see a new flier about some group or class. They're always trying something new here. If you don't go to a scheduled callout you could be infracted.

Another program is called Family Friendly. One visiting day a month, they close the visiting room and let anyone with any children on their visiting list (and without restrictions against minors) come to the visiting room. The staff sets up different booths of crafts and games that you and the kids can do together. It is nice to be able to bond with your kids in a way you can't in a normal visit.

This place has a lot to offer to those who want it. The programs are well taught and prisoners take them seriously. They have a good library department that will go out of its way to help you find what you're looking for. The staff is friendlier than in other places. The last three prisons I have been to, have been good to me.

Because most prisoners here have short sentences, their outlook on life is different. They're either just coming into the system or just leaving, and if someone is willing to sit and listen they can learn new things. Most of the prisoners here want help and are getting help. There are many programs that long-term prisoners can take advantage of. It is harder in some ways, because I'm not going home soon and I see all these people coming and going, but if I keep myself focused I can take advantage of my minimum custody. Tomorrow I could be somewhere else.

Jason Suydam

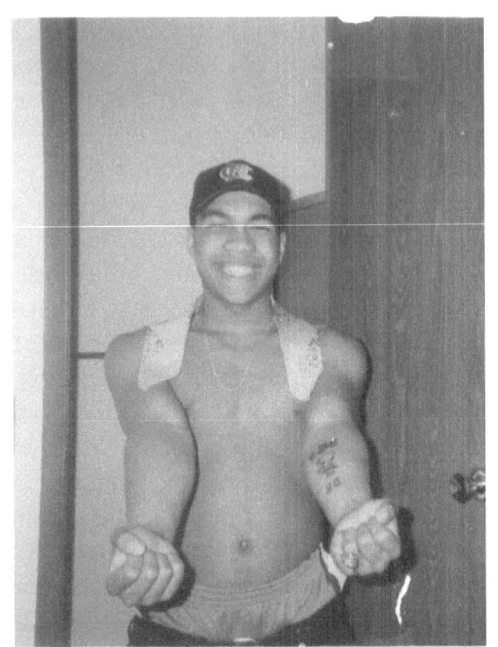

Samuel Turner (prior to prison)

Samuel Turner 2007 (present)

Lawrence Johnson

Bill Van Court

Matthew Wright (Author) present 2007   Matthew Wright (Author) before prison
1992

My Family (clockwise top left) Dad,
nephew(Wyatt), Me, Sister(Dora),
Niece(Evelyn) mom(Roberta)
deceased

My little sister (Katie) deceased

My Family (clockwise top left)
Dad, sister(Dora), sister(Katie),
Mom(Roberta) and Me(Matthew
Wright)

Katie Wright (1996)

Programming Opportunities

In the Washington State Department of Corrections, every prisoner has to have a high school diploma or GED before they're allowed to work or attend any of the schooling programs. Once they show proof of a diploma or GED, they can start to explore all the wellness classes, programs, and jobs the prisons offers.

For all the everyday basic jobs, you're paid $0.42 an hour with a $52 monthly limit. Positions include kitchen workers, custodians, porters, janitors, clerks, recreation workers, grounds crews, and assistants.

Some prisons have state-run correctional industry factories that offer skilled work positions where you can earn up to $1.10 per hour. Most of the jobs are making basic prison supplies for institutions, but others are sold to other state-owned facilities. Some of the jobs available are license plate making, prison laundry washing, dry cleaning of staff uniforms, making office dividers, assembling and upholstering computer chairs, making state-issued clothing, mattresses, and pillows, and making signs for parks, highways, and freeways.

Every prison contracts through a different local community college in its area to have teachers and classes brought into the institutions. All the prisons have self-help groups and volunteer programs. The schooling and programs vary from place to place. Every teacher and volunteer has his or her own way of teaching, so every class you attend is different.

The classes the Department of Corrections offers include Keyboarding, Computer Basics, Adult Basic Education, English as a Second Language, Information Technology, Poetry, Writing, Parenting, and Multimedia. They also have the self-help groups Anger Management, Chemical Dependency, Victim Awareness, Alternatives to Violence, Fitness, Stress Management, Job Readiness, Job Dynamics, and Alcoholics and Narcotics Anonymous.

At some prisons, they have vocational training classes that will train and certify you for a work trade that you can use after your release. Some of the certified courses are custodial services, plumbing, roofing, framing, dry walling, welding, and computer and electronics repair.

There are many programs throughout the year that volunteers come in to instruct, including religious studies, book reading clubs, Words Travel (reading children's books on cassette tapes for kids), weightlifting competitions, Veteran's

Action Group, Community Aid Coalition (making arts and crafts to donate to charities), Long Distance Dads, and Toastmasters.

The recreation departments all offer yards with walking/running tracks, pull-up and dip bars, soccer and softball fields, weight decks, and basketball and hand-ball courts. The gyms have basketball and handball courts, exercise machines, a weight deck, pull-up and dip bars, and punching bags.

Every prison has legal and regular libraries. The legal library offers typewriters, legal research materials and books, basic supplies, updated court decisions, generic forms, notaries, and current resources/information books.

The library has current magazines and newspapers; resource books for release information on grants, jobs, and housing; paperbacks; hardcover books; and access to interlibrary loans.

The mental health department has social workers for one-on-one counseling and psychologist for mental-health evaluation and treatment.

Every prison has a visit room where you and your loved ones can sit down and socialize a set number of days a week. Most prisons have Extended Family Visits (EFVs), in which your family can come into a manufactured home on the prison grounds and spend a couple of nights relaxing and enjoying private time together.

Prisoners can witness and experience terrible violence, pressure, gang-style environments, loneliness, and a severe lack of privileges in prison. Other than the schooling and programs that prisons offer, most prisoners have only each other to live and learn by. The world that I made around me is what sent me to prison. This is the same for every prisoner.

The Department of Corrections is an institution geared toward punishing pris-oners rather than rehabilitating them, but if someone took advantage of all or even some of the programs that prisons offer, they could learn a lot about themselves and others—responsibility, self-discipline, work skills and crafts, communication skills, and patience. They could get into good shape mentally and physically and gain more self-control over their anger, stress, and lives. There's a lot of help avail-able to those willing to look and listen.

Prisoners' Stories

Jason Suydam

The prosecutor's recommendation was 240 months; my defense attorney and the top sexual deviancy therapist in the state recommended 6 months jail and intensive outpatient therapy. The judge did not agree with either counsel. "This man has cooperated completely and passed every polygraph, but he cannot just be released after only six months. I cannot merit a 240-month exceptional sentence, nor can I merit a 6-month term. "My decision is 160 months in the Washington State Department of Corrections, and ordered to complete the sex offender treatment program at the Twin Rivers facility in Monroe."

So off I go. My name is Jason Suydam. I was twenty-one when I got locked up, and the past nine years have been a journey I thought I would never take.

The number one concern with all sex offenders in prison is paperwork. Any time you go to a new prison, you will be asked for your paperwork, and I had none. My second concern is that not only am I a sex offender, but I am a gay man. I didn't come out or even tell anyone about this until I reached Twin Rivers about three years into my sentence.

The R-units were actually not too bad. No one asked many questions about my crime. When I was asked, I had a story about an assault charge that I made up to keep them happy, and it seemed to work while I was there. I did three to four weeks in R-3, then moved to R-5, where I stayed for about three months. I was there so long because I had two major infractions—one for possession of money totaling more than ten dollars. I had about twenty books of stamps, and they considered that currency. My second infraction was a 603, for possession of a controlled substance. I had someone's pills from medical on me. This was not too good of start for my introduction to the prison system.

Now I had no custody points and I was required to do two years in a closed custody facility. My choices were Clallam Bay or Walla Walla, and I had heard bad things about both places. Clallam Bay was known as the Gladiator School, and Walla Walla was known as one of the toughest prisons in the country. I figured I was screwed either way I went. I choose Clallam Bay, as it was the closer of the two for my family.

When I got to Clallam Bay, I was assigned to B-unit red pod. About ten minutes after I got to my cell the biggest and ugliest white dude knocked on my door. I about shit my pants when I looked out and saw who it was. I went out to the pod and he asked me what I was in for, and I gave him the story of my assault. Then he asked to see my paperwork. I told him that I didn't have any—my attorney had it until his bill was paid off, but my mother was working on sending me something. He told me that I had one week to get it here or things would be taken care of in a different way. In about a week, I got a letter from my "attorney" that my mom made up on nice paper; it talked about my "assault charge" and how I should take the current plea deal. So I took it out and showed the big white dude, and he looked over it and said cool and I was all right with all of them. I guess these guys are not here for being smart, I thought. This may be easier than I was worried about, but I knew better than that.

Looking back, I should have asked all of them to bring their paperwork out along with mine, but I was a young kid and felt very intimidated. Some people viewed me as a weak person because I was so quiet and didn't cause any problems. Now that the paperwork thing was taken care of, I was somewhat less concerned.

I had a very high-profile case and was on the news and in every local paper in King and Snohomish Counties. I was always worried about it coming back up in the news or being in the paper. Every time the mail would come around and the newspapers came out, I worried that something would come out, and I always listened to their yelling on the tier, to see if it was about me. I was a very quiet guy then and did not like any altercations at all, definitely not physical altercations. So, I was always looking over my shoulder.

I stayed pretty much to myself, but I eventually had a crew of people around me that I hung out with and went to the yard and gym with. One of my best friends there got me into power weightlifting. I got pretty big, but my self-esteem still held me back from being who I could be.

I eventually got a job in the chapel. It was more a place for me to hide who I was and put a front on to everyone else. I definitely didn't want anyone to know I was gay or a sex offender, so this was good place for me to hide.

After a year or so, I ended up getting a job with my friend in the plumbing department. This was a good change after sitting behind a desk for so long. Now I could go around the entire institution, even to places other inmates couldn't go.

I did two years in closed custody before I was eligible for medium custody. I definitely took advantage of that—anything to get out of closed custody. I moved out to the medium custody building and moved in with my good friend, who got me the job in the plumbing department.

On February 6, 2000, I was napping in my cell and about 5:20 PM there was a knock on my door. My entire life in prison was about to change. The officer at the door asked me to come with her to the sergeant's office. When I got there, I saw three officers, two sergeants, and the shift lieutenant. The lieutenant told me to turn around and cuff up. I asked why, and they told me to cuff up first. So I did, and then asked what I did. They told me that I did nothing, that King 5 news did a report on me, and a sergeant at home saw it, called the lieutenant, and told him to get me out of population. I had no choice in the matter; I was now under involuntary protective custody. I tried to explain that I would be all right, but they said no, and I then spent a five-month stretch in the hole. During that time there was discussion of where to send me; out-of-state options even came up. This was when my family really became involved. They found out about Twin Rivers Unit at the Monroe Correctional Complex. Finally, after five months, I ended up going to Twin Rivers.

When I got to Twin Rivers, I realized that I should have been here a long time ago. Eighty percent of the people here are sex offenders, so people don't really care what you are in for. Even though I was in a better place, it took me a little while to relax and get used to this place. When I hear people running towards me, I still turn and get ready for somebody to sock someone. Eventually I relaxed, and it got to be a pretty nice place.

I started working in the Recreation Department just a few months after I got here. I am a clerk, and I schedule all the games with the Recreation Supervisor and plan all the special events. It's an okay job, because I can set my own hours and work when I want.

Up until now, no one in prison had known that I was gay. At least I thought so at the time; now I know that people picked me out as soon as they saw me. That was the other secret I never wanted anyone to know about me. It came out in the middle of a summer volleyball tournament. I am actually so glad; it feels like a weight has been lifted off my shoulders. I can actually be myself, and my self-esteem has been building since then. I get more respect now that I have come out than I ever did when I was in the closet.

About homosexuals in prison: there are gays, faggots, and I guess queens or broads. Gays are your average guys, who you may or may not even be able to tell are gay. They may be in a relationship, but they are the most conservative of all the homosexuals. They are in it more for the emotional aspect than just sex. But don't get me wrong—the sex is also pretty important. This is the class that I put myself in.

The queens or broads are exactly what they sound like; they try as hard as they can to be like a woman. Many of them actually go to get the big cut done when they get out. I feel the big reason they do this is they think if they look and act more like women, guys in here that haven't had a chick for a long time will actually go for them. They will do anyone anytime without a care in the world.

The faggots, which also include queens, will screw anyone anytime whether they have any diseases or not. They don't give a second thought about anyone or anything they do. It is all about where they can get their next cock.

Some people may fit several of these categories, but this is basically it.

I have now been at Twin Rivers for about six years. I have been working in the education department for the past four years, doing computer graphics and vinyl sign and banner production. This sign department is the only one in the state, and it is the best job I have had since being locked up. This is actually something I would like to do when I get out, and this job is giving me the skills and practice that I need.

Being out for the past six years has made my time more interesting here. I am locked up in a prison with eight hundred other guys, and I am not able to get away from them or have my privacy. It's a lot nicer when you have someone to be with and share your time with. Many people wonder why anyone would want to add to the drama of everyday life in here by being in a relationship. Most of it is the companionship and being close to someone you know you can trust. Most people in a gay relationship in prison, including myself, are co-dependent people. Being in a relationship gives them the comfort and security they need.

The prison staff does not condone inmates being in relationships. They will usually not stop you from doing it, but any outward signs of affection are not allowed. Here the bigger concern is the other prisoners and their gossiping. In other prisons, everyone pretty much does their own thing. If you walk by a bathroom and someone is getting beat up, you turn your head and keep walking and say nothing. At this place, there are jealous people and snitches. They get into everyone's business and feel it is their duty to spread gossip or tell on you. It is still hard for me to understand it.

I got locked up at twenty-one years old, and I have about two and a half years left on my sentence. My young adult life was spent in prison. When I got locked up, I heard about people being institutionalized, reaching the point where they are so used to this place, this is all they know and do not want anything else. I said that will never happen to me. But nine years later, I am looking at getting out in a couple of years and thinking, holy crap, can I really do this? I know that I will be able to do it, and I really am going to do everything I can to make it work.

Prison itself does nothing to rehabilitate you. Even when I go to the Sex Offender Treatment Program next year, they only give you the tools to make a change. It is up to the individual to make the change.

I missed a good part of my life in here. I missed a lot of my family life; all my brothers are married and have kids. Yes, life still goes on while I am in here. So now, I will do whatever it takes to get out of here and use the tools they have given me to stay out.

Am I scared? Absolutely. This has been the best thing that has ever happened to me. It may sound crazy, but prison has slowed me down and made me look at my life and take inventory. Prison changed not only my life but also my family's life. If you ever find yourself in such an unfortunate situation, remember two things: yourself and your family. Those two things are ultimately what matter and what you live with the rest of your life.

This has been the best learning experience of my life. My family and I learned many things over the last decade. The most important of these is love for your family.

Samuel "C-Mike" Turner

As far as stress and fear are concerned, sentencing and arriving at prison were the worst moments in my life. Between the judge and the wall of prison, it's hard to decide which is more intimidating. Even though I took a plea agreement for thirteen years, I was shocked when the judge said, "I hereby sentence you to one hundred and sixty-two months." Telling my family and wife of six months was the hardest thing I ever had to do. I'll never forget watching my mother chase after my wife.

The reaction of the courtroom was overwhelming. It's one thing to say you love someone, but showing it is another. I knew my family loved me unconditionally, but after seeing their reactions, I felt it. I cried that day; it was the first time in my whole life I ever felt completely helpless. No amount of money or support could help me. I was devastated, not necessarily by the moment but because my life up to this point consisted of making money and supporting my family.

In my opinion, I wasn't a bad person. I'd had my share of trouble here and there, but I don't think what I did warranted a thirteen-year sentence. Politically, drug dealers and gang members are society's ailments. God forbid one of them gets shot while breaking the law. Victims are those who are victimized. If you are a victimizer, how can you be victimized? I'm not saying what I did was right or should be accepted; I'm just commenting on the logic behind the state's decisions concerning citizens and criminals.

Once sentenced, I found relief knowing I was finally on my way to prison.

Upon arriving at Washington State Reformatory, my emotions and fears became erratic. In one instant I was scared; then I was anxious. The fear was the result of uncertainty. The anxiousness was due to the stress of the trial lifting and realizing it was time to embark on a new chapter in my life.

The first thing I noticed after getting processed in was that behind that menacing wall was another world. People were everywhere—streams of bodies, hundreds of people, all moving at once, each doing his own thing. It was shocking to see. From the outside looking in you see a facility that looks small, with a huge wall, but on the inside it was enormous. Prison has a fully functional world that the outside world is oblivious to, with everything from a church to a college.

After finding my cell assignment, I had the rest of the day to explore my surroundings. The first place I went to was the Big Yard. I figured if I had any problems this was where they would surface. The Big Yard was packed, with perhaps a few hundred there. People were everywhere, playing everything from bocce to basketball. Scanning the yard, it was easy to see the segregation. Every race and cultural group had an area. After looking around a bit, I saw a familiar face. To most that would have been comforting, but I was a gang member and the face I recognized was that of one of my enemies, "Blue" from "Hoover."

As nervous as I was about being in prison, seeing him gave me relief. I knew he knew me, so I used our status as enemies as proof that I was tough. Nonetheless, our meeting went without incident and we quickly become allies.

After meeting the "homies" and learning the ropes, prison began to get comfortable.

Seeing fights was alarming at first, but I soon figured out that fighting comes with the territory; it was "prison diplomacy."

For a gang member in prison, everything is political. Things as simple as finding a seat in the dining hall were complicated. All the rules that you were supposed to follow as a gang member on the streets but didn't for whatever reason were now strictly enforced. Don't snitch, don't be soft, and stay loyal to your crew. At any time, something could happen.

On one occasion, an African American got into it with two young skinheads over the volume of their music. It wasn't that big of a deal, but everything in prison gets amplified by ten. Usually if you're in the gang world "loop," you get to know all the illegal activities going on. This day was different, because I had been at a visit with my family all day. I was on my way to the gym to pick up my weight room card. In the gym, I saw a lot of fellow gang members grouped up in the corner in a circle. Being curious by nature, I figured I would go over and see what was happening. Ten to fifteen whites stood in the middle of the circle, and from my vantage point, they appeared to be arguing. The next moment, everyone started fighting. In prison, especially with gangs, there is a code of ethics everyone must follow. I had to help the troops in war. Everywhere you turned there were people fighting. If you were of another race, you were an enemy. This was a turning point in my life, because I realized how ignorant I was. I didn't even know why we were fighting. All I knew was that if I didn't fight, I would be beaten up later by the "homies."

In prison, leaders are driven by greed; greed motivates everything. It is rare to meet someone in prison that has your best interest at heart. People in prison are desensitized. After a few years you begin to realize you can't trust or depend on anybody, family included.

Visitation is to some the light at the end of the tunnel. It's the only source of good to balance the evil. A visit from your family in most cases makes you forget about the world inside. I've seen some of the hardest criminals turn into lovable teddy bears in visits.

However, visitation has a dark side. When someone comes to visit you, they are considered guilty until proven innocent. Everyone is suspect. In my eight years of incarceration I've seen everyone from grandmothers to babies caught trying to smuggle in contraband. To combat contraband, the DOC (Department of Corrections) has many rules. Although they exist to insure the safety and security of the prison, they can be intrusive and embarrassing annoyances.

On one particular occasion a friend of mine's wife was on her way to visit and saw another prisoner's wife walking to the prison. She offered the lady a ride, being nice and knowing they were going to the same destination. After arriving at the prison, the ladies were processed in. As they were, the drug dog had a reaction to the ladies as if they were carrying drugs. (Usually the dog sits wherever he smells drugs.) The ladies were searched, both their persons and their vehicle. During the searches, the correctional officers found nothing. Afterwards the ladies were not allowed to visit and were ultimately barred from visitation for a minimum of ninety days. The ladies didn't have anything, but in prison there isn't any benefit of the doubt. This can happen to anyone.

Most prison drugs are brought in during visitation, usually by people known as mules. Anyone can be a mule. In the gang world, mules tend to be the weak. Usually the mule is coerced into trafficking for the betterment of his or her community or gang.

In most cases, being a gang member involves being a follower, and in some instances that means repressing your personality and or opinions. Gang members and organizations alike have what are called "mission boys." Mission boys are the people who beat undesirable individuals. Undesirable individuals are snitches, sex offenders, and PC cases (protective custody). All it takes is one person saying or hearing the wrong thing about you or your court case to put your life in danger.

I've seen enough during my eight years of incarceration to scare a man straight. I've seen attempts on people's lives, drug overdoses, suicides, rapes, and a host of other offenses.

Is prison like the movies? No! Movies don't show the pain and the struggle. Movies don't show the hand of God. Movies don't show the support the community has for felons. Movies don't show the transformations.

When I first fell in 1999, I was a menace to society. I shot two rival gang members. In gang terms, that's almost the equivalent of being a war veteran and surviving. In my frame of mind, I didn't feel as if I had committed any offenses. What I did to come to prison was almost a reward for not being killed on the battlefield, as so many of my peers had been.

I used to attribute my plight to being fatherless and to circumstance. Now, as a fully coherent adult, I'm leaning towards the idea that if I had a better choice of role model in my community, things might have been different. This is not to downplay my own decisions, because ultimately I chose my own destiny.

Many consider my life a success story. I've come a long way from the immature being I was almost a decade ago. Many people have "gambled on me" and my support in the community has increased dramatically because of the changes I've made. As a future member of society, I feel as if my newfound change is slowly becoming addictive. A lot of inner city youth come to prison assuming I am the same person I was when I was on the streets and naturally tend to look up to me. When they see someone as corrupted as I was be the person I am today, I become that role model that I needed when I was growing up.

A year or two ago I heard a quote. "There's never a testimony without a test." I didn't quite understand it at the time, but now I know this was my test.

I am married, as I have been for the past eight years, and have a baby boy on the way. I am currently training to be a network administrator/teacher's assistant, and I sincerely participate in all programs available to make me a better member of society. My hobbies are rapping, working out, and coaching in the prison's intramural basketball league. I'm twenty-eight years old and still have the rest of my life to look forward to.

Bill Van Court

As I write this, I have been back in prison for the past twenty-four years. This is my second time in prison as an adult. I served six and a half years my first stretch.

My name is Bill Van Court, and I am a lifer in the Washington State prison system. My father was an alcoholic who often physically and emotionally abused my family. I became rebellious at an early age, and it did not take me long before I began getting in trouble.

One of the main contributing factors to my re-offending was my continuous drug and alcohol use. I started drinking whatever booze I could get my hands on at around age twelve. At age fourteen, a neighbor kid and I started sniffing glue a lot. By age seventeen, I was smoking weed, taking speed, and dropping acid.

At that time in my life, my drug use seemed like fun. The other young kids I was hanging out with were doing it and it seemed like the "cool" thing to be a part of. I remember working at a few odd jobs, but I never kept any job that long. I would get a paycheck and then just piss it away partying with my friends, then be hung over going back to work.

I'd already been in trouble a lot as a juvenile for car theft and petty burglaries. I was stealing money or other people's property just to sell this stuff and would spend the money on more drugs or alcohol.

By age eighteen, I'd been introduced to "crank," or speed, and I started mainlining. All the other drugs I did before this time became boring, I guess, but shooting speed was a real jolt of adrenaline. When I first started using it I felt I could do anything, but all I really did was stay awake for a couple of days at a time talking all kinds of stupid shit with other people I got high with.

After using speed for some time, I got pretty strung out for a number of years. I lost a lot of weight, felt sick most of the time, and got a lot of cavities in my teeth. A big downside of speed is eventually you will do just about whatever it takes to stay high. I know many people, including myself, who would steal from anyone—friends and family, it didn't matter—just as long as they could get high again.

I'd get involved in a relationship with someone, but I'd put my drug use first and could never quit using for long. As a result, my relationships would never last. I was too selfish to think about another person's needs or desires.

At the age of twenty-six, I got into some serious trouble with the law and got sent to prison for the first time. I was sent to the Washington State Penitentiary, in Walla Walla, Washington, where I served six and a half years before being paroled. My first day in the joint, I didn't know what to expect. Little did I know I was in for a big wakeup call. I soon found out that drugs were as rampant today in prison as they were on the streets, if you knew where to look.

It didn't take me long before I was using again. At first, I was selling off the little bit of personal property we were allowed to have in prison and then begging my family for money.

One day, while I was sitting in my cell on the third tier, someone a few cells away started screaming at the top of his lungs. I took my little square mirror and stuck it out of the bars on my cell door so I could see down the tier. Three prisoners had this guy under a blanket on the walkway of the tier. They were repeatedly stabbing this guy with shanks, knives they had made in prison. They killed him and walked away.

A prison guard must have heard the screams, but no guards came to his rescue. I found out later that he was killed for welching on $10 drug debt. This man lost his life over a stupid petty debt. The guys who killed him were never caught.

Seeing this guy killed was a horrible sight. I'll never forget him screaming for his life. I was thinking one of his killers might have seen me looking down the tier with my mirror. Shit! They might decide to take me out to. I kept my mouth shut and went about my business, doing the daily boring prison routine, and no one ever approached me about it. That's the way things operate in prison. As harsh as it sounds, survival was a top priority in a place like Walla Walla.

Over the next six years, I continued to use drugs and was caught by the prison staff only once. I made sure I never got into debt with anyone. During my stay in prison there were at least four other killings, and one guard was stabbed to death.

The prison was on lockdown half the time I was there, it seems. Four men crammed in a tiny cell twenty-four hours a day without ever getting showers, and cold TV dinners shoved under the door three times a day.

Summertime in Walla Walla stays close to one hundred degrees during the day, and we had no air conditioning. The flies were everywhere because no one was allowed out of their cells to take out the garbage or shower.

Being from Seattle I hardly ever got a visit from family or the few friends I had left. The prison was just too far away, as are most prisons. I think that's one of the hardest things you face being locked up, being away from the people you really care about.

Near the end of my first term in prison, when the guard was killed, the whole prison rioted afterwards and the guards assaulted many of the inmates, destroying much of our property in retaliation. The killing and rioting resulted in a six-month lockdown of the prison.

There are many tough men and women in the prison system who play off doing time as easy. But believe me, that's just a front. No one likes being in prison and everyone wants out. The big problem is that many people just can't seem to get out and stay out, including myself.

When I was finally released the first time, after doing six and a half years, I was really happy. I felt like I'd just gotten home from a warzone. I swore I would never get in trouble again.

Within two weeks of being let out on parole, I started drinking again. Just a few beers almost every day while I was out looking for a job. Within a month I started smoking weed, just to take the edge off the stress I was feeling trying to fit back into a world I had been away from for so long. These were the excuses I used to give myself permission to use again.

Someone introduced me to a woman they thought I might hit it off with. Turns out she liked getting high as much as I did, and within three months I had jumped my parole and she and I were living together. Because I wanted to get high and party a lot, and because I was now on the run from the law again, I made no effort to work. Instead, I went out and started pulling burglaries and robberies again. I was back to using speed again, and this only gave me a false sense of courage and clouded my mind enough so that I did not have to think about the people I was hurting.

Between getting high and committing more crimes, I got my girlfriend pregnant. It was the worst possible time. I was about as irresponsible as a person could be. Here I was going to be a father of a child for the first time, and my whole world was falling apart around me. I felt more pressure than ever and continued to keep getting stoned and committing crimes.

After being out of prison only six months, I got arrested after getting into a police chase. I was linked to most of the crimes I was pulling and charged with six new serious offenses. After going to court I was sentenced to two life sentences and three ten-year sentences, all running consecutively, meaning I would serve one sentence after another.

My son was born when I was sitting in jail waiting to get sent back to prison. The first time I saw him was from the other side of a glass partition at the county jail visiting area. I didn't even get to hold my only son.

After that first year in the joint, my son's mother left me and hooked up with a heroin addict. Soon after she got hooked on heroin, got in a serious car wreck while she was high and our four-year-old son received a bad skull fracture and came close to dying. My sister ended up adopting my son and raising him on her own.

I have been back in prison for twenty-four years now. I've watched from afar as my son grew into a man. We never spent any time together as a father and son in the free world. The only time I've gotten to see him is in a prison visit room. It is always under the watchful eyes of the prison guards and cameras in the ceiling of the visit rooms.

All the rules and restrictions of prison make it impossible to really enjoy a visit. The last time he made the trip here to see me, he was denied entry because he was wearing shorts, as it was a hot day.

Visitors are pat searched and must clear a metal detector before coming into the visit room. Another time my eighty-three-year-old mother was a denied a visit because the back of her blouse was silk and the guards could see her bra strap. For

Christ's sake, she's eighty-three years old! But this is how prison staff treats our families. They view them as criminals and treat them as such just because they're coming to visit us.

I feel bad about putting the people who love and care about me through the ordeal of visiting me. I'm angry at the prison system for the unfair way they treat innocent visitors. I put myself in this position, though, so I'm mainly responsible for all the consequences.

Ten years ago, I finally stopped using drugs. Since I stopped, my life has become more manageable. I can wake up in the morning without needing a hit of something to see me through, and I can spend the money I earned from working on things that bring me a more lasting pleasure than a quick fix or temporary drug high ever did.

It hurts me to the bottom of my soul that I may never get out of prison. The worst part is not being home with my son and family members. There is nothing in this life worth the loss of your freedom. Being in prison is the next worst thing to being in hell, and for some people who die in here it can be their living hell.

My wish is that all the young people in the world realize the pitfalls of drug and alcohol abuse and realize that violent behavior is not the answer to resolving things. We all just want to be happy and live peaceful lives. This is what I feel.

Laurence Johnson

My name is Laurence Johnson, but I am known by Washington State Department of Corrections as #286348. I have been incarcerated now for fifteen years and am set to be released in 2027.

I wouldn't wish the managed lifestyle I've experienced on any parent or teenager. By the time I'm released, over 90 percent of my time will have been spent in prison. That is, however, if I can make it through this medical nakedness (by which I mean *neglect*). For all the inmates that populate Twin Rivers Correctional Complex (about eight hundred), there are three medical providers. You do the math.

Before coming to prison, my yearly salary was over $50,000 working as a house painter. Drugs were my downfall. I was a user with a habit bigger than my income could keep up with, so my criminal activity was a result of my usage, and prison the result of it all.

Prison has been my mother, father, and God when it came to educating me to be a better man. It's was not the system itself that made me a better man as much as the realization of my own mistakes and choices; now I have the time to reflect on what putting myself in this position has done to myself and my family.

In the end, it's my life that has to change for the better. As far as the Department of Corrections is concerned, there is no profit in trying to rehabilitate me or anyone else. It's like putting money in the bank without the interest.

Syndicated columnist Neal Pierce from the *Seattle Times* says, "Many of us are sure to despise the finding. Isn't the overriding reason for jails and prisons to lock up the bad guys and protect the rest of us? Aren't we the country that decided, beginning thirty years ago, to substitute punishment for rehabilitation? Haven't we demonstrated our toughness by imprisoning 2.2 million people—the most of any nation on earth? And pumping up our prison and jail expenditures to a stunning $60 billion a year? So now you're telling us that bad stuff is seeping out of jails and prisons and back into our neighborhoods, cities and towns? Well, yes."

So you see, it's about the money, not the man.

As a free man, a lot of thinking from day to day is not required, because you know what it takes to keep things running smoothly. You are responsible for every move, good or bad. Well, the bad finally found me, and my reckless behavior took me to the breaking point. The result was my next place of residence, where I would learn a new kind of lesson.

This lesson was different from any I experienced as a kid, teen, or adult.

The jailhouse wasn't so bad, but I will say this about being in jail—it was full of hate and lots of unpredictable men with uncertain futures, making for a hostile new environment.

After thirteen months of mental grind, uncertain hope going through trial, and thinking about my own fate, I understand the pain I caused the people directly in the path of my destruction, not to mention my family and children, who have been affected by the choices I made as a young man. Once sentence, and I was on the next chain to the receiving units, and then on to the big house, Walla Walla, a prison called the most notorious in Washington.

Here I encountered a completely new type of treatment. After getting off the bus, I was told to take off my jumpsuit and was sprayed down with some kind of lice repellent and then given a set of clothing. The unknown, the next move, filled me with fear. They put in a room only to guess what was next.

What came next wasn't so bad; however, there were still many fearful expectations ahead.

Unlike the real world, where you have daily plans to make things go smoothly, this place is a controlled environment. You're told when to eat, sleep, and shower. You couldn't even use the restroom without three other guys present.

In my new world, I've seen things people outside these walls and fences would never want to see or even imagine. Here behind these walls, men are forced to live together. That itself is inhuman. Sure you might be thinking, "That's what you deserve," but that's until you have a family member who's been good all his life but one day drives down the road at 100 MPH drunk and kills a whole family. Now it's "Please, have mercy on my boy!" Well, I'm someone's son who made a really bad choice.

My lesson is in my face every day that I wake up and look through a bar door, waiting for someone to say, "Mainline." Every time I am confronted by a racist skinhead or some big, buff white guy with "white" on the back of his left arm and "pride" on the back of his right arm. Every time an officer says to me, "Lift up your privates and turn around and crack your butt."

So, if you, society, think for one second that I'm not paying for my bad choices, think again!

It's not about self-pity anymore; it's about getting through these long years alive. It's about learning to respect human life and being responsible as an uncle, brother, and father.

Prison is a place where they prepare you to become a productive citizen in society. The alternative is succumbing to its destructive pain, harboring thoughts of revenge and hate, and becoming bitter.

Johnni H.

I am in prison because I believed all of what *they* said and how *they* defined me. Know this: I take full responsibility for my crime. This is not a debate, but it is part of my story, a story about you, about your best friend, your little brother who looks up to you but is too scared to be honest with himself and you and so he hides. It's about your older brother, too concerned about the image he must uphold for you to look up to. It's a story about one of humanity's deadliest flaws—*pride*. Rather than admit the truths, whatever they might have been, we chose a life of duality, a life submersed in carefully categorized boxes, a life in the closet. This, all because of pride. Can you even believe that?

I got six years in prison—doing four—because of pride. Now, that is idiotic of me, yet it is common. I should have known better, been better, especially given everything *they* taught me. I even heard comments like, "You could have told me" and "You should have just sought help." Oh yeah, that's all I needed to do. What was I thinking? That would have been so much easier. *Wrong!* That is why living dual lives has forced more teens and adults to the brink of self-destruction, via drugs and alcohol, crime, and suicide.

I was recruited to play college football for the University of Washington. Awesome, huh!? Or I could have wrestled for one of the greatest wrestling coaches of our time. Cool! But did I really even like sports? Of course I did. *They* told me so.

I was a naturally gifted speaker, had excellent communication skills, understood people, and was extremely comfortable in social settings. I was a good public speaker, motivator, and coach of people. I believed in the goodness within people—I fought racism by educating people through public discourse, intimate conversation, and debate about real change.

Dynamic and energetic, *they* called me, the Energizer bunny and the sunshine king. *They* said I had a promising future.

Coach and mentor to business leaders twice and three times my age, generating and instilling the courage to fail, try again, adapt to change, persevere, excel, achieve, create, imagine, and dream, a guiding light to live the lost. Coach of young men, developing and growing, good quality young men through athletics, teaching young men to mature as positive, productive, healthy members of society, guiding the wayward away from a life of drugs and alcohol.

Talented businessman, salesperson, manager of people; innovative and creative.

Destined, *they* would say, for greatness, mainly because of an insatiable achievement-driven work ethic founded on a determination to be the best. *They* had their optimism and placed me on top of an extraordinarily high pedestal.

Married to the perfect woman, soft and gentle yet strong, like a beautiful wildflower.

I tried to fit in and live up to *their* expectations, honestly. I tried! We even had a house with a dog and made food for the neighbors.

That was me, my life designed by *them*, another poster child rising up from the trenches of poverty to success. Raised by a single mom, a star athlete, successful teacher and coach, public speaker, innovative and effective businessman. Sounds pretty good, huh? It was all built on a shaky foundation *they* helped build, through mentoring, guiding, teaching, and coaching—a foundation built on distortions and misrepresentations.

As the falseness of this existence became clear, the house of my life began to sway, shatter, tumble, and eventually collapse.

I was a gay man with a wife playing the superbly organized and defined role of a straight man. The beginning, the first tremor, began when I separated and eventually divorced from my best friend, my wife. The unraveling began. Life as I had seen it since as far back as third grade was crumbling. Reflections of a hidden life—my demons, the skeletons buried deep in a lonely, heavily locked closet—began to appear. Scared of the truths, the horrors I would face, I hid behind more work, long hours and numerous projects, and during my free time, sex with anonymous men.

While preparing to have quick sex with this guy with whom I'd had previous encounters (one of my fuck buddies), I inquired about some "smoke," seeking marijuana to ease my stress and ultimately run from my depression. He had smoke, but it wasn't marijuana; it was crack cocaine. Since I had never done anything besides marijuana, I did not think to ask about why we were smoking out of a glass tube. All it took was one hit, and I was addicted. My closeted self, repressed for so many years, was free to play. It started about two times a month and only at his place. Then he introduced me to certain Web sites for PNP (party n' play), sex clubs, and his friends. Then it was every weekend, then any free time, until it—the addiction to the drug and the freedom it provided my other self—began to invade the other life, the life *they* saw. My addiction started to move into my daily life of work, a cohabitation of sorts.

As my two worlds collided and life as I knew it was crumbling, along the way I made a choice that eventually led to drug-related charges.

Prior to these charges, both worlds could not exist in my head. The collision caused a category-ten tremor, which led me to the edge of a bridge contemplating my existence. I wanted it to cease, but since you are reading this, you can guess that life looked better than death. I have never been a quitter—always a fighter, a finisher, a solution finder. Prior to being charged or even knowing I was going to be, I moved to a different city for a business opportunity and started learning to live one life instead of two. It was new and refreshing. Then I was charged and sentenced to prison. All this because of pride. If I could have, I would have just told someone.

But I didn't. instead I kept silent and had sex (and lots of it) with different guys, all the time with lots of crack, a dash of alcohol, and some other drugs I don't even recall. No one knew, no one suspected, until it was too late and I was charged, sentenced, and taken to prison for drug charges. The straight superstar athlete with the looks, the girls, the popularity. How could he be on drugs? No way, not him. There has to be a mistake.

I can still hear my mom yelling, screaming, and crying, being dragged out of the courtroom after the judge sentenced me. That was very sad to see and a very sad memory to recall.

The worst part is, even though I have grown from the whole experience, I am still addicted. Even after everything, I am still addicted. Granted, I am a recovering addict now, but I still have to live with the craving every day. Each day I have to wake up with the positive self, talking about being sober today even though I know deep in my heart I really enjoy the sensations I get while smoking crack.

The prison experience is … it is what it is … but in the end, in prison, it is just you! New choices arise even before you get the chance to reflect, feel, heal, and repair or improve from your last and most recent mistake. Just as in life, choosing not to choose is still a choice. You will choose a path to take, a path of solitude or a path of a group. Are you going to side with the Aryans, skinheads, blacks, Natives, Mexicans, a gang? Are you going to do drugs, going to peddle them, going to sell yourself for food, clothes, drugs? Are you going to be in a gang? How are you going to do your time?

Once you figure that out—your next steps, your next year or decade—*you must decide* if you are going to stand up for it *or* you will adapt yourself to each new situation in order to survive. Will pride continue to force your hand? Will you continue to be driven by *them*? Do you have the intestinal fortitude, the testicles, to be you? These are the questions you face from day one! The rules of prison are different. Learn them fast or pay for it.

Time to get off the chain bus, shackles off, single file to get paraded through the processing center naked. Tag your weight, height, number, and location of any tattoos, clothing sizes, DOC identifying number, and tons of other paperwork, then into your orange jump suits. You get a pair of shower shoes, a pair of walking shoes with Velcro straps, used socks, used underwear (hopefully you don't get a stained pair), and a T-shirt. You line up for showers, standing there with more than a hundred other inmates in your underwear or towel or sometimes naked. You get five minutes in the water and five out to dry, then back to your cell. You shower in a line with five to six other guys. You get to shower every other day. If you need to bathe other than that, you have to take a birdbath in your cell, with your cellmate there with you. At the receiving center, you are on twenty-three-hour lockdown, except for meals, a drastic change from freedom. Throughout this intake of experience, you learn the main points of the prison code (in no particular order):

1. it is *them* (corrections officers/DOC) versus us (inmates),

2. look the other way,

3. stick to your kind (race, gang, clique), and

4. mind your own business.

One of my first associates in prison had done about four decade of time, all but three years in the California corrections system. He had been a leader of the skinheads at several prisons, had done a seven-year stint in a shoe program, and to top it all off his body was covered with skinhead, white pride, and Swazi tattoos from the top of his neck to the end of his toes. The tattoos were visible even with a high T-shirt on. At first glance you might assume he was still a skinhead, but when we met he was a born-again Christian whose life had been saved by a black man. That event changed his life. He told me I was his first black friend. Being of mixed race, having both black and white friends was not new to me, but the two of us walking in the chow hall caught everyone's attention. He got pressure and so did I. I had a threat placed on my life—someone passed a message on to me that if he and I continued to associate, I was going to get shanked. Eventually people stopped harassing us, because neither of us was going to be swayed.

Playing a game of pinochle while taking a break from work (we were all porters for the unit), I was introduced to the idea of words being a reason to fight. And I thought I was long since past elementary. This day, I called my partner a punk for making a dumb play. Now mind you, the five other guys I worked with were all white guys with some affiliation to white power, white pride, or skinhead groups. My partner jumped on top of the table and was frothing at the mouth. I had no idea what his problem was. They all explained it to me. They also made it very clear we were not going to have to fight, me versus all of them, because since it was just us there, they had nothing to prove. *They* are so invasive, everywhere! Another rule, you are supposed to fight if you are called out—called a punk, bitch, fag, or boy, among other names. If you don't fight, you will be fought by *them*!

On top of all the other issues and changes, you had to deal with the fact that visits with family and friends are done through glass and phones. Eventually, if you moved units prior to heading to your new institution, you were allowed in-person visits, where just hugging someone becomes an awesome, blessed experience. Human touch is vital, something I took very much for granted when I was free.

One of the hardest experiences I went through early on in prison was realizing I had zero control over outside situations with family or friends. My family went through crisis after crisis shortly after I came to prison. I was normally the go-to guy, but I couldn't help. I felt so sad and down. At one point, a close family member passed away. I was in a state of shock and at a loss for what to do. My heart ached, mostly for my other family members but also for the loss itself. Shortly thereafter was the funeral, and I was transferred to my new institution, a new place to learn and adapt to.

Life goes on as normally as it can in prison—you play some pinochle and bones, go to the gym and play some ball, lift weights, hit the bar work, walk the Big Yard, chop it up with the homies, and so on. Then tremors from the past, from my other life, begin to rumble. I meet someone, an outted gay man and a sex offender to boot. This was not intended; in fact, it was not supposed to happen! I was only in my second month at my institution, a place where I would most likely spend my entire time. What to do, what to do. *They* started to question, started to wonder what I was up to, and so *they* assumed he was just my punk.

I had too many skeletons in my closet and had seen too many lives lost to lies and deceit. By this time, I had realized I was in prison because of this, my pride. I decided, no more! I was not going to live a lie any longer, and I was not going to try to shove a man I was interested in, who was out of the closet, back into the closet by keeping our interest in one another a secret. I would no longer be a part of that. Though I was not ready to make announcements to the compound, I did not hide my interest in him.

"We" were heavily scrutinized in the beginning. Most of the problems we incurred came as subtle comments and harsh looks from other inmates and even some staff. Though staff cannot overtly speak or act out against homosexuals or those they believe to be homosexual (since they work for a state organization that does not "officially" tolerate discrimination of any sort), corrections officers find a way to share their views.

Aside from being two men noticeably attracted to each other and hanging out together (lifting, working, socializing) we were different races, one white and one black. This was a problem in prison, an even bigger one than being openly gay. But we stayed the course and made it through.

However, even now we are a topic of conversation, for many reasons I imagine. One reason could be the length of time we have been together, three years. Another reason could be that our release plans are intertwined, as are our families. It could be that many people straight and gay seek us out for relationship, business, and other advice. It could be so many reasons. But I do know this: when new arrivals come many times they know us before we know them, thanks to the ever-persistent drama brigade.

During this same time I started to acclimate myself to the environment, figuring what my daily "program" was going to be. One of the most frustrating aspects of being in prison is finances. This is a good example of prison as a microcosm of society. Finances are always at the heart of life's struggles, even for the rich. It is only a matter of perspective. In prison, though, your income is only forty-two cents per hour, not to exceed $55 per month. Yet cost of living is the same as if you were on the outside, and sometimes more. In addition, jobs are almost non-existent. My institution, like others around the state, had industry type jobs when I first arrived. But due to a host of heated debates in the state legislature, industries were removed from all Washington State prisons. The debate was about the companies involved having an unfair advantage, because they had to pay inmates only minimum wage instead of a prevailing wage. On average, the difference was $13–$18. In the end, shortly after I arrived in prison, jobs were scarce.

Though time passes efficiently, many aspects of prison life cause hiccups, disrupting the program. One of these hiccups relates to health care, medical and dental. The system is a byproduct of the bureaucracy that supports it. It is cumbersome, backward, and ultimately inefficient and ineffective. Lawsuits filed against DOC for healthcare-related issues are massive and numerous. In addition, DOC loses the majority of those cases, costing the taxpayers billions. But DOC seems not to care, because the system still runs the same, shitty, and inmates die because of it.

Imagine waking up in the middle of the night sweaty, in pain. Your throat feels as if it's closing, and what breath you can take is painful and forced and the Energizer bunny is playing its drumbeat commercial on a looped repeat. In the free world, facing such extreme pain (beyond simple discomfort), you would immediately go to the emergency room. However, in prison, since you are not dying or about to die, you will have to wait until the morning sick call. If you think you are in enough pain that you might be dying, you can push your emergency button in your cell and declare a medical emergency. You push a little button, and then the on-duty CO comes to your cell and asks what the problem is. As long as you are breathing and not sprawled out on the floor, you do your best to explain your symptoms. While doing all your explaining, he is getting very pissed—he is at your cell because he is, after all, a state worker, and this little situation is going to create a lot of additional paper work for him. Forget that you could be dying. After a considerable amount of discourse with the CO, he notifies main control and medical that an inmate has claimed a medical emergency in such and such unit. At that point, additional officers and appropriate medical staff are dispatched to your cell. They take you, if you are still alive, to medical for a look-see. If by chance you are just super ill—let's say a temperature of 105 degrees and reduced breathing space—and thus are not dying, you will be returned to your cell with a major write-up for declaring a "false" medical emergency. So, it's a tossup: declare a medical emergency and take the chance of getting a write-up or don't take the chance and maybe die. And yes, I have seen it happen. In one situation, the guy called for the CO in the middle of the night, they had the conversation about his breathing, the CO said it didn't sound like a medical emergency, and thus in my opinion he talked him out of declaring one. In the morning, after I had returned from breakfast, they closed our wing down because the guy had died in his sleep. Sad. A huge lawsuit followed and DOC lost.

Sick call is another sad joke. You are never sure when the sign-up sheet is going to be up, and when you get seen it is by a nurse who cannot prescribe anything for you, not even over-the-counter medication to reduce swelling or inflammation or to make it easier to swallow water or breath. Very sad and frustrating. The nurse just tells you to sign up to see your provider, which is in fact *not* a doctor but a physician's assistant (PA). He or she will hear from you only for fifteen minutes and one issue at a time. After you go to sick call one morning, you try to sign up for the next several days, and finally, three days later, they put up a sign-up sheet. Luckily for you, you have an appointment to see your provider in nine days, in which time you will probably be feeling better or have had to declare a medical emergency, and so the cycle goes.

Dental is not much different, except when you do get in and get seen, their goal is simply to fill your cavities with temporaries and pull the really bad ones. Not good.

I was in prison when I learned I had HIV. Though I was devastated, shock kept me from dealing with my emotions for a long time. I was terrified. When I first got here, I had seen a guy who had HIV. He was pointed at, mocked, made fun of, and of course ostracized. This scared me into silence. I felt I had no one to turn to, and so I did not until much later. When I finally did, it was not on my own terms. I confided in a cellmate who then confided in his "special" friend. To make matters worse, that "special" friend was an enemy of mine. He was very pleased to learn of my predicament and devised a plan to share it with the entire institution. Thus, my HIV status became well known. In the end, I became stronger because of it and I learned an important lesson: *Trust no one in prison!*

As I previously mentioned, prison is a microcosm of society and therefore is separated into groups or cliques, and the gay community is no different. Yes, there is even a gay community in prison, but it sucks for the most part. There is such a broad range of homosexuals in prison that continuity or even a basic sense of community is hard to attain (and is usually not all that desired). There are tough-guy "fellas," street homies, and other straight-guy personas who overtly talk down about gays in front of their friends and even physically threaten them. Those same men are having homosexual sex in the confines of their cells or in some other discreet location. There is the prison "punk," who is protected from physical harassment but who loses all dignity and self-respect in the process and is often passed around within the clique or community that owns him. There are the truly gay and out, who exhibit the stereotypical characteristics of the effeminate gay male. They are often harassed for being themselves and *not* taking on the persona of a "punk." Then there are those like me, who try not to be defined by the categories *they* have established. Though I am a gay man who is in prison for a drug addiction, HIV positive, and with his life-partner, those characteristics do not define who I am. I am my own man, defined by my habits, attitudes, beliefs, and actions.

I am in my final leg, the final stretch of my time in prison, preparing for release, preparing to go home. I have learned a great deal about prison and how it operates both on the surface and at its core, behind the scenes. Mostly, though, I have learned a great deal about who I am and how to live life for me, not for *them*. Prison was a good pause for me, but not necessary. I could have accomplished this tremendous personal growth without coming to prison, but then again I might not have. I used to be on a career course chasing the next great opportunity, the next achievement, always moving forward without reflection. I have learned to pause, slow down, reflect, improve, and then continue. I am a much better man now.

Katie's Story

I had been sitting on the cold, wooden bench, probably for a couple of hours, when I looked up to see cameramen running towards the courtroom entrance. It all happened so fast I did not figure it out at first. Then I heard what the commotion was about. The jury had a verdict. I quickly asked my sister and her friend if they would make a trip to the bathroom with me. Once I got into the bathroom stall, I said a quick prayer. "Please Lord, let them acquit my brother." We then quickly ran back to the courtroom. Once we got into the room, there was a quiet hush as my shackled brother was escorted in with two King County Court House security guards on either side of him. News cameras lit up the area, filming Matt, and then dimmed while they waited for the jury to arrive.

Those were the longest five minutes of my life, as I sat in the courtroom with my heart pounding almost through my chest. Finally, I heard a door open. The jury slowly filed in. They all looked at my family. I just could not read their faces. The bailiff then said, "All rise!" and we stood. The judge entered the room. We sat down. While the judge asked the foreman if they had reached a verdict, my sister's friend grabbed my hand. So did my best friend, Sandon. The courtroom got silent as the verdict was read. I remember thinking that everything came down to this moment. Nine months of agony, and in one second our fate would be changed.

"We, the people of the state of Washington, find the defendant, Matthew Byron Wright, guilty of the murder in the first degree of Audra Letnes."

I only remember hearing a gasp of shock from the many lawyers sitting behind me. I became numb and felt tears rolling down my cheeks as each juror stood to confirm their vote on the verdict. The news cameras continued to record the entire situation as my family sat in shock, crying, and my brother was then shackled and led out of the courtroom. I remember trying to tell Matt that I loved him as I watched him leave. I then followed the rest of my family as we left the courtroom into the hallway. There I could see a smiling prosecutor talking to the reporters. Once the press saw my family, they immediately headed our way. My mother cried "No comment!" but they continued to badger us. Attempting to find refuge from the news people, I followed my family to a hallway that led to the bathrooms. So did the cameras. And they just stood there and filmed us cry. This had been the culmination of one of the most significant events of my life: my brother's accusation and conviction of the murder of Audra Letnes. I was emotionally, socially, and even spiritually affected by this horrendous tragedy.

Life turned into a nightmare once Matt became a suspect in the murder. My worst fears were put to the test, and I never realized how scary life could be. I was forced to live in a house full of fear and under constant attention. I could not escape what had happened, whether it was attending the same school the victim did, where rumors ran rampant, or turning on the evening news to find the newest update on the case; I was placed under the most pressure I had ever felt in my life. As a result, I ate less, had problems sleeping, and lived in constant fear. At one moment, I would think things could not get worse, and the next day they did. This still affects me today. Whenever life is stable, making me feel happy and safe, I get scared. I am afraid to trust life and be distraught and frightened as I was before. I know now not to take happiness for granted, because what we have in this moment might be gone in the next. It has been hard for me to learn that we can trust the world.

While my emotions have been placed on trial during this ordeal, so have my friendships. Tragedy has a tendency to either bring people together or split them apart. As soon as my brother became a suspect in the murder, I learned very quickly who my friends were. The character of my family became a debate, and my friends were forced to judge this situation. With every person I become close to, I have to explain a part of my life that is hard to comprehend. I never know what reaction I can expect or how the person will treat me after learning of the murder. When I meet people who are native to the Shoreline area or attended any of the schools that my family members or I did, I am always faced with the difficulty of people realizing the relationship between Matt and me. Usually, I get the same response of both shock and curiosity, and I then always wonder what the other person's opinion of me is. That is why most of my current friends are very open-minded people who try not to judge any situation too quickly. I value them greatly.

As I had to deal with the emotional and social perplexity of the situation, I was also forced to grow spiritually as a person and take a different outlook on life. Politically, everything seems to affect me. While prison reform has become a hot topic on the news, it now takes a personal note. Every time I hear a politician state that prisoners have no rights, I can only think of my brother, hoping that people will try to see the situation from all angles. I also learned the necessity to read the newspaper and be updated on all social issues of the day. One small decision from the Supreme Court could drastically affect the outcome of Matt's appeal. I am also proud to say that I am extremely tolerant and always attempt to see all viewpoints. People's reactions towards me have taught me that not everyone in life has the same values or background that I have. I know the importance of making others aware that they are good people and will be accepted regardless of what they have done or said. I just try to respect others as I have only hoped to be respected.

I now have a better understanding of the meaning of life and God because of what I have been through. I feel there has to be some larger purpose for all the pain and suffering I and many others have felt. I know at some point in my life something positive will result from this whole ordeal, and I have a strong belief in fate and our roles in it. I have reprioritized my values and am able to reflect back now to how life once was for me. I regret the moments where I could see my brother outside the restraining walls of a prison, with no limits on how long we were together. If I could change the past, I would have tried to know my brother for the person he was. But I am using this experience as a lesson towards how I treat others. While I still have many things to learn, grow from, and change, I'm trying to make the best of every moment spent with the ones I love. Because Matt is no longer a regular part of my life, I am trying to make the best of the limited time we have together. I can honestly say that I am just lucky to have him alive, safe, and able to talk with me. I also will never be able to forget Audra Letnes and what she meant to this world. For whatever pain and suffering I have gone through, nothing will ever be able to compare to the loss of those who loved her and knew her most. Life is not always fair, but living each day to the fullest is the only thing each of us can do.

Conclusion

Every prison is different but every prison is the same, a prison is not just a prison. There is so much going on besides what we do to each other. Everything is cold—the ground, the walls, the people, the policies and procedures—everything is de-humanized.

A prison never sleeps. Every second of every day there's something going on somewhere. Screams, arguments, fights, pressure, empty stares, drugs, tattoos, strip searches. Nothing stays the same, but nothing changes.

A prison does not call you up and ask you to come over and play; a prison is forced to take you. I know that every prisoner would say bad things about prison, but the truth is you make your own prison. I did not want to live in or around a closed custody facility for ten years, but I know why they sent me there. Prison has never done something to me that I did not cause myself. I don't hate prison. I needed prison.

There's so much going on in prison but also so much to be had. I've had a lot of bad years in prison and I've caused myself a lot of grief. When my sister Katie died, I remember going into the dayroom and seeing everyone talking shit and playing the same games, watching each other, telling the same stories over and over again, and I knew I was no longer a kid. I was done with all the games and ready to be an adult. One day I am going home, and this will not be my life. What I do today is how I will be remembered tomorrow.

Prison is the best thing that ever happened to me. My family has always been here for me, and no matter what I do or say, they keep coming back. I got to spend time with my sister, which I wouldn't have if I wasn't here. After she died, I started really listening and talking with my family and I saw a different side of life I never knew.

My family started sending me books, magazines, work documents, articles, newspapers, and clippings so I could see what they think and do and that there's another world out there. I started reading, writing, exploring, and I can't wait for any opportunities to learn and make my life and the lives of those around me better.

I always thought that everything was about me; I didn't know that we all need each other to live and learn. My family has come every week or more since I've been in prison, because they need and love me. I owe it to them to do everything

I can to make our lives better. I will never lose an opportunity to spend time with my family again. There is nothing more important.

Although prison has been a good experience for me, this world sucks and I would like people to know that. This life does not end; people keep coming and going, and it never changes. It gets easier as you go down in custody levels, but it doesn't get better. In closed custody, the people are the same as in medium/minimum custody, but in medium/minimum custody there is more to lose so the prisoners hide behind thicker masks.

I've spent all my adult life in prison, but prison is not my life. I don't care how people judge me anymore, because I like me. I don't need to impress or prove anything to anyone; I don't have anything to hide. I'm thankful for every day I have done in prison and I will never forget what prison has done for me.

The Goad

Through all my madness and all my sadness,
I learned how to pull my strings.
How I pull them and how you judge them
Is never how it seems.

The puppet master who pulls faster
Does to make amends.
He plays the demons and his best friends
To make a change within.

The puppet master who's through with laughter
Is trapped in his own sin.
He has his madness and his sadness,
But he cannot win.

Appendix

CLOTHING

Item	Description	PR/ MIN	MED	CLS	MAX	REC	VALUE (Each)
Athletic Support	Standard design	2	2	2	0	0	10.00
Belt	Plain leather or cotton mesh; open buckle no larger than 2"x2"; unlined	1	1	1	0	0	20.00
Coat, Winter Weight	Heavy lining; hoodless;no longer than mid-thigh; no zip-out linings	1	1	1	0	0	100.00
Gloves	Foul weather full finger;cloth or knit only; no padding; no leather	1	1	1	0	0	12.00
Handkerchiefs	White only	5	5	5	0	0	2.00
Hat/Cap	Stocking; Baseball	2	2	2	0	0	15.00
Jacket/Coat, Light	Light lining; hoodless; sweaters/sweatshirts with zippers, snap, or button front; waist length	1	1	1	0	0	50.00
Long underwear	Standard two-peice set; top and bottom; no one-peice	2	2	2	0	0	30.00 set
Pajamas		2	2	2	0	0	25.00 set
Rain Coat	Clear Plastic	1	1	1	0	0	
Robe	Standard waist tie; 3/4 length only	1	1	1	0	0	50.00
Shirts	No 'half shirts" or mesh type; no epaulets	3	3	3	0	0	25.00
Shoes/Boots	Sneakers; boots; derss shoes; 6" inch or less from bottom of shoe to the top of shoe/boot; 1" or less heel thickness; all shoes must pass metal dector	3	2	2	0	1	100.00
Shorts	No tight fitting, i.e spandex, lycra, or other elastic material; no cutoffs or altered; no less than 4" inseam	2	2	2	0	0	20.00
Slippers		1	1	1	0	0	20.00
Socks	Standard crew or calf length; gym or dress; pair	7	7	7	0	0	3.00
Suspenders	Elastic; 1 1/2' maximum width clip end only	1	1	1	0	0	20.00
Sweat cloths	Top; standard pull-over crew or v-neck Bottom; standard drawstring/elastic waist; elastic or open ankle; no jogging suits	2	2	2	0	0	35.00 set
Sweater	Knit pullover; crew or v-neck	1	1	1	0	0	35.00
Trousers/pants	Pants/jeans; straight leg or boot cut; no tight fitting; no invisable pockets or reversable pants; no cargo pants or pockest on legs	3	3	3	0	0	40.00
Undershirts	Standard; short sleeved; plain white T-shirt; crew or v-neck	7	7	7	0	0	5.00
Undershorts	Regular briefs or boxer shorts	7	7	7	0	0	5.00

PERSONAL PROPERTY MATRIX
Men's Facilities

HEALTH CARE ITEMS

ITEM	DESCRIPTION	PR/ MIN	MED	CLS	MAX	REC	VALUE (EACH)
Glasses, prescription and/or contacts	All glasses and contacts in non-metalic cases	2	2	2	1 Glasses only	1	
Sunglasses	Non-reflective type; no mirrored	1	1	1	0	0	20.00

JEWELRY

ITEM	DESCRIPTION	PR/ MIN	MED	CLS	MAX	REC	VALUE (EACH)
Earring	Post type only; no gems/stones; no larger that 8mm	1pr	1pr	1pr	0	0	15.00 pair
Medallion	2"; no gems/stones (religous only in IMU)	1	1	1	1	1	50.00
Neck Chain	24" maximum; no gems/stones	1	1	1	0	0	50.00
Wedding Band	No gems/stones; only authorized if offender is married	1	1	1	1	1	100.00
Wristwatch	Time; day; date; alarm and stop functions only; no gems/stones	1	1	1	0	0	100.00

MAJOR NON-CONSUMABLES

ITEM	DESCRIPTION	PR/ MIN	MED	CLS	MAX	REC	VALUE (EACH)
Alarm Clock	Wind-up only	1	1	1	0	0	20.00
Electric Fan	12' maximum size	1	1	1	0	0	25.00
Electric Razor or Hair Trimmer	Non-rechargeable	1	1	1	0	0	50.00
Headphones/ Earphones		1	1	1	0	0	20.00
Radio/Cassette	AM/FM radio and/or cassette player/recorder; single cassette only; maximum size allowed is 18"x10"x6". Walkman type with headphones allowed	1	1	1	0	0	70.00
Television; No remote	Must be portable with earplug or earphone attachment capability; screen size 13" maximum	1	1	1	0	0	Inmate Store
TV Cable	Maximum length 6 ft.	1	1	1	0	0	
Typewriter & Accessories	Portable; electric, manual, or memory (no disks or memory expansion card, maximum memory of 32k); no battries allowed; limit 4 ribbons with the machine and one spare print apparatus/wheel	1	1	1	0	0	300.00

PERSONAL PROPERTY MATRIX
Men's Facilities

MISCELLANEOUS

Item	Description	PR/MIN	MED	CLS	MAX	REC	VALUE (Each)
AC Adapter	One for each approved electrical device						
Ash Tray	Plastic only	1	1	1	0	0	
Bowl	Plastic only	1	1	1	0	0	
Brush, hair	Plastic only: one peice	1	1	1	0	0	
Caculator	offender store purchase only	1	1	1	0	0	
Cards, Deck (Playing)	Standard and Pinochle	2	2	2	0	0	
Cassette Head Cleaner	No solvent-based cleaning fluids	1	1	1	0	0	
Cassette Tape Holder	Plastic only	1	1	1	0	0	
Cassette Tapes	Clear case screwed or glued; or glued opaque; pre-recorded commercial tapes; blank tapes; or authorized letter tapes	20	20	20	0	0	15.00
Comb/Pick	Plastic only; no rattail	2	2	2	0	0	
Cup/Tumbler	Plastic only: no thermal or insulated unless clear	2	2	2	0	1	
Ear Plugs	Noise protection	1 set	1 set	1 set	0	0	
Extension cord/Power Strip	9 feet maximum, UL approver; offender store purchase only	1	1	1	0	0	
Games	Dominos; Chess; or Checkers only	2	2	2	0	0	
Hair Dryer	1200 watts maximum	0	0	0	0	0	
Headphone Extension Cord	Not to exceed 12 feet in length	1	1	1	0	0	6.50
Mirror	Plastic; 6"x6"	1	1	1	0	0	
Musical Instrument		1	1	1	0	0	300.00
Nail Clipper, large		1	1	1	0	0	
Nail Clipper, small		1	1	1	0	0	
Photo Album	Photos only, no metal binders; not for news-paper or magizine clippings; not to exceed 8.5"x11"	1	1	1	0	0	
Pitcher	Plastic only	1	1	1	0	0	
Reading Lamp	Plastic only; Plastic clamp only	1	1	1	0	0	
Soap Dish	Plastic only	1	1	1	0	0	
Sports Awards/Plaques/Medals	State issue	2	2	2	0	0	
Tweezers	3 1/2" maximum size	1	1	1	0	0	
Y. Adapter		1	1	1	0	0	

Visiting Room Guidelines

DEPARTMENT OF CORRECTIONS
VISIT GUIDELINES

WELCOMING STATEMENT

The Department of Corrections welcomes you to <u>facility specific.</u> We wish to provide a family friendly environment. To do this, there are some security measures we must take to ensure your visit is safe and pleasant. The allowable number of visitors at one time may vary from one facility to another. All Department of Corrections facilities are chewing gum and tobacco-free. Please read and focus on the guidelines so you may have an enjoyable visit.

<u>WHO CAN VISIT</u>

Each offender may have up to <u>facility specific</u> approved visitors per visit. Note: Offender may not be available for a visit. Visitors may avoid making an unnecessary trip, or being turned away, by pre-arranging visits with the offender.

Reminder: If you no longer wish to be on an approved visitor list, please submit a request to be removed in writing.

Minors may visit with an approved escort only.

<u>WHO CAN VISIT</u>

<u>Visiting Times</u>

Where	Days	Check-in Time	Check-out Time

The offender you are visiting can make arrangements for special situations.

Visitors who leave authorized visitor areas during any visit period will be allowed to return during the next authorized visit period.

HOW YOU GET THERE

Facility Location Information (printed by facility)

- Written directions from north, south, east, or west, and a map, as appropriate.

- A contact number if visitor gets lost.

Parking Information

To ensure the safety of all, persons not visiting including children and pets must not be left in cars.

- Written instruction from parking lot to visitor entrance for check-in. (Provided by the facility)

- Physically Challenged Information—Any issues regarding parking, special accommodations, and entrance for check-in. (Provided by facility)

WHAT TO DO WHEN YOU ARRIVE

Visitor Check-in

Visitors are welcome to arrive facility specific minutes prior to visits. Once your vehicle is locked, please check-in at the visit entrance.

DOC VISIT GUIDELINES

Visitors, who must share bad or sad news, please inform staff in advance.

Identification

All visitors, 16 and older, will be asked to show current photo identification (e.g.: driver's license, passport, military or government identification, tribal identification, alien registration, student identification).

Searches

Visitors will be asked to sign a search permission form which is required for visiting. Pat searches, vehicle searches, personal property searches and/or canine searches may be conducted.

Carry-Ins

The following items must be contained in a clear plastic coin purse or plastic bag:

- Money—Each visitor is allowed $15.00 in change or bills in denominations of $5.00 or less **or** a vending machine debit card, for those facilities that have debit vending machines available.

- Keys—The drivers of vehicles may keep one manual car key on a non-charmed key ring. **Instructions where to secure keys will be determined by the facility.**

- Small comb or brush

- Medical—Visitors are allowed life sustaining medications or medical equipment that is needed during the visiting period, if the visitor provides proof or prescription of medically authorized need.

HOW TO ENJOY YOUR VISIT

The following guidelines are in place to ensure a safe and pleasant visit.

Continuation of your visit and visiting privileges will depend on:

- Arriving without having consumed alcohol and/or illegal substances or being in possession of contraband.

- Visitors and/or offender following DOC Visit Guidelines.

- Compliance with search procedures.

- No disturbances or emergency situations within the facility.

- No clear and/or immediate danger or suspicion of criminal conduct that threatens the health and safety of any visitor, offender, or staff.

Dress standards are necessary to ensure the safety and security of visitors and offenders to promote a non-offensive, family oriented environment and to provide efficient processing of visitors. The visiting Sergeant/designee will make the final determination regarding the appropriateness of any clothing. Footwear, accessories allowed. The following guidelines apply to visitors <u>five years and older</u>:

Clothing

- All clothing must be clean and in good repair free from holes, rips, or tears.

- Undergarments must be worn to include briefs and brassieres for females. Males must wear briefs, boxers, or long underwear.

- Clothing must be worn that does not expose undergarments, cleavage, stomach/midriff, bare back when arms are raised or bare chest. Examples of inappropriate clothing are: Tight fitting, low cut tops or bottoms, sheer, see-through or mesh, camisole type tops, halter tops, tank tops, sleeveless blouses or shirts.

- Dresses or skirts must be no shorter than <u>at the top of the knee.</u>

Footwear
- All visitors must wear socks, stockings or pantyhose.
- Shoes, sandals and boots must be in good repair. We are unable to allow flip flop/thongs, shower shoes, slippers, or foul weather style boots or shoes.

Accessories

- Jewelry

    o Four pieces of jewelry in piercing (e.g.: one nose, one lip, two ears or the combination of four pieces of pierced jewelry).

    o One watch.

    o Wedding ring set and one ring.

    o Two necklaces.

    o Two bracelets.

- Two pair of eyeglasses, top include one non-reflective pair of sunglasses for outside visits only.

- Belts may be worn excluding money belts or belts with compartments.

- Headgear or excessive hair ornaments, when medically required with written verification, or part of a religious practice.

Clothing and accessories listed below, or other items considered to be a threat to the security and safety of offenders, visitors or staff as determined by the Superintendent/designee, will prevent your visit.

- Camouflage, wrap around clothing, bib attire, shorts, clothing referring to obscenity, alcohol, drugs, gang references, or sex in any form, and clothing that is difficult to search (e.g.: excessive pockets, padding or layering of one outer garment over another).

- Jewelry that hides other items (e.g.: broaches, lockets, pins, or jewelry that looks like a key).

Items for infants and toddlers

Items for infants and toddlers will be carried in a clear plastic bag or container.

- Two clear plastic bottles containing water, juice, milk, or liquid formula.

- One plastic Tupperware-type child's cup with lid.

- Two unopened plastic containers of baby food in their original packaging with one plastic baby spoon.

- Two bibs.

- One pacifier or teething object.

- One non-quilted child's blanket.

- One change of baby clothing.

- One disposable diaper per hour of visit.

- Baby wipes must be transferred to zip lock plastic bag prior to visit.

COURTESY DURING VISITS

It is the intent of the Department of Corrections to maintain visiting programs which help offenders preserve positive ties with family and friends. Cooperation by all individuals is essential. The following visit room guidelines are in place to ensure that visits are a pleasant experience for all:

- A brief hug and kiss are permitted at the beginning and conclusion of visits.

- During the visit the only physical contact allowed is holding hands with hands in plain view

- Conversations should remain quiet without harsh language or swearing, encouraging pleasant and caring family interaction.

- Visit areas are provided for all visitors. Please use visit room furnishing for their intended use.

- Because time is limited, your focus and interactions must remain between your own visitors and family.

- During visitation, money or debit cards may be used for purchases from vending machines by both offenders and visitors, depending on the facility.

- Visitors are reminded to take all unused money or debit cards with them when they leave.

- Children must be under direct supervision and visual control of the visiting parent or guardian at all times, including children using the restroom. (Offenders may supervise their visiting children while the adult visitor uses the restroom.) Roughhousing and horseplay will be stopped immediately by the visiting parent.

- Verbal corrections and time-outs are the only allowable forms of discipline during visits.

- For safety and proper identification offenders will wear their identification at all times.

- Showing affection to your children, holding and playing with your visiting child promotes positive family interaction. Please remember to be considerate of other offenders and your public surroundings.

- Grooming of children's hair may be done during visits unless visits occur in dining areas.

- Please use the changing areas for children, which are provided.

- At times visits may become emotional. Should this happen, a staff may check on your visit.

- Please put away all items used during visits (e.g.: games, toys, books). Please throw trash and recyclables in containers provided at the end of your visit.

Suggestion/comment forms are available in the visit room of the facility you will be visiting.

Infraction Codes

General (Minor) Infractions

Unauthorized possession/theft

051 - Unauthorized possession of money, stamps or negotiable instruments the total value of which is less than five dollars.

053 - Possession of anything not authorized for the retention or receipt by an inmate and/or not issued to an inmate by regular institutional channels.

255 - Misuse or waste of issued supplies, goods, services, or property, the replacement value of which is less than ten dollars.

310 - Pretending or failing to take prescribed medication that the inmate has accepted by concealing or retaining a single daily dose.

354 - Theft of food, the value of which is five dollars or less.

356 - Possession of unauthorized amount of otherwise authorized clothing, bedding, or issued supplies.

Loaning/Trading

052 - Loaning of property for profit.

351 - Giving, selling, borrowing, lending, or trading money or anything of value to, or accepting or purchasing money or anything of value from, another inmate or that inmate's friend(s) or family the value of which is less than ten dollars.

Altering/destroying property

055 - Mutilating, altering, defacing or destroying any item valued at less than ten dollars and that is not the personal property of the inmate.

Disruptive behavior/lying

202 - Abusive language, harassment or other offensive behavior directed to or in the presence of staff, visitors, inmates, or other persons or groups.

203 - Lying to a staff member.

244 - Unauthorized displays of sexual affection with another inmate.

353 - Disruptive behavior.

355 - Horseplay, roughhousing or any other unauthorized physical contact between inmates.

357 - Unauthorized demonstration, practice or use of martial arts.

Failure to follow rules and orders

102 - Failure to follow any written rules or policies adopted by the institution and not specified within this chapter or in local disciplinary rules.

103 - Refusing or failing to obey an order, oral or written, of any staff member.

210 - Out of bounds; being in an area where the presence of the inmate is unauthorized.

214 - Interfering or failing to comply with count procedures.

251 - Smoking and possession of tobacco products.

301 - Failure to keep you person or your quarters in accordance with institution rules or policies.

Unauthorized communication/visitor contact

303 - Unauthorized use of mail or telephone.

304 - Unwanted written and telephonic communication to any person.

305 - Correspondence or conduct with a visitor in violation of published or posted rules and policies.

309 - Unauthorized display of affection with a visitor.

Inappropriate use of equipment

212 - Using any equipment or machinery when not specifically authorized or contrary to instructions or safety standards.

Unexcused absence/feigning illness

104   -   Unexcused absence from work or any assignment, scheduled meeting, appointment or call-out.

352   -   Pretending to be ill or injured contrary to medical/mental health screening results.

Inappropriate sexual behavior

328   -   Possession of any written, photographic or hand-drawn material that depicts a sexually explicit act as defined in WAC 137-28-160.

DEPARTMENT OF CORRECTIONS

CLASSIFICATION REFERRAL

REVIEW PERIOD: 03/16/94 TO 04/14/94   FACILITY / LIVING UNIT: WCC/RC   plk

1. REFERRAL AGENT:	REPORT DATE:	2. MXED:	3. NRD:
MARIO O. LUENGO, CC III	04/14/94	06/05/2036	04/95

4. REVIEW OF CLASSIFICATION FOR:

[X] INITIAL (RC)	[ ] Camp	[ ] W/R	[ ] ISRB
[ ] Six Month/Annual Review	[ ] Ad Seg	[ ] PPR	[ ] Transfer
[ ] Other (specify)			

5. NARRATIVE:

PROGRAMMING: Reception Center test results indicate Wright has a BETA IQ of 106 and functions above the seventh grade level. Program recommendations should include ABE with receipt of high school diploma, stress/anger management, vocational training, and advanced academics for AA and BA business degree. Wright communicates in the English language.

SERIOUS INFRACTION RECORD: Past: None.
                                  Present: None.

MEDICAL: The Health Status Report, dated 03/24/94, indicates Wright has minimal medical and dental needs.

MENTAL HEALTH: Wright claims to be dyslexic. He states he participated in the Northwest Mental Health Program in Seattle, Washington from ages 11 through 16. He reports his involvement with the mental health program was due to his parent's divorce and his trouble with the law.

COMMUNITY SUPPORT: Wright lists his family and girlfriend as community support.

COMMUNITY RELEASE PLAN:

   PRIMARY RESIDENCE/ALTERNATE: Wright states he has no current release plan.

COUNSELOR COMMENTS: Wright is a determinate sentence inmate currently serving 34 months and 494 months - consecutive - on his first and second adult felony convictions. Wright has an ERD of 04/02/2030 and an ICD score of **26**, which equates to **Close Custody**. Community placement is ordered with special conditions. Wright owes $549.80 in legal financial obligations.

INMATE COMMENTS: Wright prefers WSP, where he will enroll in adult basic education classes for his high school diploma and then advanced academics for a business degree. He states he needs placement at WSP for he needs to be separated from various gang members at CBCC, due to previous problems.

Per V. Lynch offender can be assigned either WSP or CBCC

RECEPTION CENTER CLASSIFICATION RECOMMENDATIONS/ACTION: DATE:

Custody Close

                                                    Cannon 4-18-94

DIVISION OF OFFENDER PROGRAMS RECOMMENDATIONS/ACTION: DATE:

                                              Close CBCC

                                              Stewart 5/3/94

6. DOC NUMBER	NAME: LAST	FIRST	MIDDLE
709976	WRIGHT,	Mathew	B.

DOC 5-30(REV. WCC 10/92)   PAGE 1 OF 1

04/20/1994   COUNSELORS NAME: BR98 LUENGO, MARIO

```
| I.    DOC CRIME CATEGORY:                                    *
|                                                             *
|       A. ...........  0                                     *
|       B. ...........  5                                     *
|       C. ...........  10                                    *
|       D.* ..........  20                                    *
|          *(INCLUDES PAROLE VIOLATIONS)                      *      SCORE =  0

| II.   HISTORY OF VIOLENCE:                                  *
|                                                             *
|       A. INSTITUTIONAL:                                     *
|          - ANY INFRACTION EQUIVALENT TO (501,              *
|            502, 521, 553, 601, 602, 650, 651, 801,         *
|            802, 817, 819, 821, 853,870, 871) = 0           *
|          - NONE = ................................. 10     *
|       B. OTHER:                                             *
|          - OTHER VIOLENT CONVICTION = ..........  0        *
|          - NONE = ...............................  5       *      SCORE = 10

| III.  DETAINERS (INCLUDES POTENTIALS):                      *
|                                                             *
|       FELONY DETAINER =  0                                  *
|       INS DETAINER = ..  8                                  *
|       NONE = ...........  10                                *      SCORE = 10

| IV.   ESCAPE HISTORY:                                       *
|                                                             *
|       ANY WITHIN THE PAST TEN YEARS = 0                    *
|       NONE = ..........................  6                  *      SCORE =  6

| V.    AGE:                                                  *
|                                                             *
|       UNDER 29 = ..  0                                      *
|       29 OR OLDER = 6                                       *      SCORE =  0

|       CUSTODY:                                              *   TOTAL
|                                                             *   SCORE = 26
|       0 - 37 = CLO     38 - 47 = MED     48 + = MIN         *
|                                                             *   CUSTODY = CLO
```

| OVERRIDE/REASON: | ASSIGNED CUSTODY: Close   5,3,94
| | BY: _____
| | CHIEF OF CLASSIFICATION/DESIGNEE   DATE

    DOC NUMBER: 709976   NAME MATHEW B. WRIGHT

DEPARTMENT OF CORRECTIONS

CLASSIFICATION REFERRAL

RECEIVED
MAR 15 1995
CBCC Records Office

ACKET:
[ ] TRANSFER
[ ] COMMAND MANAGER
[ ] HCSC
[ ] CHIEF, CLASSIFICATION & TREATMENT
[ ] OVERRIDE
[ ] IMS

[ ] NO ACTION REQUIRED/FILE

REVIEW PERIOD: _3/16/94_ TO _2/15/95_ FACILITY/LIVING UNIT _CBCC/B Unit_

REFERRAL AGENT:	DATE	(P)ERD:	NRD:	MAX ED:
R. Nielsen, CCII	2/16/95	4/23/2030	3/96	6/26/2036

REVIEW OF CLASSIFICATION FOR:

[ ] INITIAL (RC)   [ ] Camp   [ ] W/R   [ ] Board
[X] Six Month/Annual Review   [ ] Ad Seg   [ ] CPR/PPR   [ ] Transfer
[ ] HCSC   [ ] IMS   [ ] Override
[ ] Other (specify) _____   [ ] No Action

NARRATIVE

PROGRAMMING: Inmate Wright was admitted to the system on 3/16/94. He arrived at CBCC on 7/13/94. During this review period he has programmed for all but one month as a student. He is not involved in any self help groups here at CBCC. He spends his leisure time in recreation.

SERIOUS INFRACTION RECORD:

7/29/94, (507), CBCC: Inmate Wright completely undressed in the dayroom. Exposing oneself constitutes a WAC 507.
SANCTION: 50 DLGCT, 5 DDS

MEDICAL: No medical or dental health services were provided or required at the time of this report. Inmate Wright is not currently taking any medications.

MENTAL HEALTH: No mental health services have been requested or provided during this reporting period.

COMMUNITY SUPPORT: Inmate Wright states that he receives visits, letters, financial support and makes phone calls to family members only.

COMMUNITY RELEASE PLAN: Upon release inmate Wright intends to reside with his mother, Roberta Wright. Her address is 19623 14th Avenue, NW, Seattle, Washington 98177. Her telephone number is (206) 546-6226.

COUNSELOR COMMENTS: Inmate Wright is serving an SRA sentence with an ERD of 4/23/2030. He owes 24 months of community placement upon release. He owes $449.80 on an active King County charge and $100 on a future King County charge. He has a custody score of 58 points which normally indicates minimum custody, however, his custody will remain close per policy due to his crime. I recommend maintain close custody per policy, retain at CBCC and that he continue to program as a student.

NUMBER	NAME: LAST	FIRST	MIDDLE
709976	WRIGHT,	Matthew	

DOC 5-30 (REV. 4/93)

Page ___ of __

REVIEW PERIOD: __3/16/94__ TO __2/16/95__ FACILITY/ LIVING UNIT __CBCC/B Unit__

UNIT TEAM COMMENTS/RECOMMENDATIONS:

DATE OF MEETING: 2/21/95

STAFF PRESENT: CUS Schouviller, CCII Nielsen, Sgt. J. Ahrens

INMATE COMMENTS: Inmate Wright indicates that the report is correct as written and has no additional comments.

UNIT TEAM COMMENTS/RECOMMENDATIONS: Unit team notes that Wright has not been a management problem during this review period. Per policy he must be retained at close custody.

1.   Maintain close custody per policy.
2.   Retain CBCC.

RN:kmm

_____   2-27-95
UNIT TEAM CHAIRMAN   DATE

REVIEW COMMITTEE:

Concu

_____   3-6-95
REVIEW COMMITTEE CHAIRPERSON   DATE

SUPERINTENDENT:

Concur

Roberta Shaw   for Mr. Wright   3-9-95
SUPERINTENDENT   DATE

6. NUMBER	NAME: LAST	FIRST	MIDDLE
709976	WRIGHT,	Matthew	

DOC 5-30A CONT. (REV. 12/87)

Page _____ of _____

ACKET:
[ ] TRANSFER
[ ] COMMAND MANAGER
[ ] HCSC
[ ] CHIEF, CLASSIFICATION & TREATMENT
[ ] OVERRIDE
[ ] IMS

[ ] NO ACTION REQUIRED/FILE

RECEIVED

MAR 14 1996

CBCC Records Office

REVIEW PERIOD: 2/15/95 TO 2/15/96	FACILITY/ LIVING UNIT	CBCC/B Unit			
REFERRAL AGENT R. Nielsen, CCII	DATE 2/27/96	(P)&RD 4/25/30	NRD 3/97	MAX ED 6/26/2036	

REVIEW OF CLASSIFICATION FOR:

[ ] INITIAL (RC)   [ ] Camp   [ ] W/R   [ ] Board
[X] Six Month (Annual Review) [ ] Ad Seg   [ ] CPR/PPR   [ ] Transfer
[ ] HCSC   [ ] IMS   [ ] Override
[ ] Other (specify) _____   [ ] No Action

NARRATIVE

PROGRAMMING: Inmate Wright was admitted to the system on 3/16/94. He arrived at CBCC on 7/13/94. During this review period he has programmed as a Student until 12/95. He was on cell assignment and waiting lists until 2/9/96. He is working currently in Food Service. He is functioning at a 7.9 grade level. He is a case managed inmate. He is not involved in any self help groups here at CBCC. He spends his leisure time in recreation.

SERIOUS INFRACTION RECORD:
   9/11/95, (657) CBCC: Inmate Wright was found guilty of four general infractions in a six month period.
   Sanctions: 5 days D-Seg suspended 60 days.
   3/14/95, (701) CBCC: Inmate Wright was loud and disruptive in the Library.
   Sanctions: 30 days loss of library privileges.

MEDICAL: No medical or dental health services were provided or required at the time of this report. Inmate Wright is not currently taking any medications.

MENTAL HEALTH: No mental health services have been requested or provided during this reporting period.

COMMUNITY SUPPORT: Inmate Wright states that he receives visits, letters, financial support and makes phone calls to family members and friends.

COMMUNITY RELEASE PLAN: Due to the length of his sentence inmate Wright has not formulated a release plan at this time.

COUNSELOR COMMENTS: Inmate Wright is serving an SRA sentence with an ERD of 4/25/2030. He owes 24 months of community placement upon release. He has a custody score of 58 points. However his custody will remain close due to his current conviction. I recommend maintain close custody, retain at CBCC, and that he continue to program in food service.

NUMBER	NAME: LAST	FIRST	MIDDLE
709976	WRIGHT,	Matthew	B.

DOC 5-30 (REV. 4/93)

Page _____ of _____

UNIT TEAM COMMENTS/RECOMMENDATIONS:

DATE OF MEETING: 2/27/96

STAFF PRESENT: CUS Schneider, CCII Nielsen, Sgt. McGarvie

INMATE COMMENTS: Inmate stated the report was accurate and had nothing further to add.

UNIT TEAM COMMENTS/RECOMMENDATIONS: Unit Team notes that Wright has not been programming satisfactorily, however, is not considered to be a management problem.

1. Maintain close custody. (MUR)
2. Retain at CBCC.

RN:jls

_____Schneider, CUS_____   2/27/96
UNIT TEAM CHAIRMAN   DATE

REVIEW COMMITTEE:

Concur

_____M. Cash_____   3-12-96
REVIEW COMMITTEE CHAIRPERSON   DATE

SUPERINTENDENT:

Concur

_____Steven R. Sowen for R.L. Wright_____   3-13-96
SUPERINTENDENT   DATE

6. NUMBER	NAME: LAST	FIRST	MIDDLE
709976	WRIGHT,	Matthew	B.

DOC 5-30A CONT. (REV. 12/87)

Page _____ of _____

PACKET:
[ ] CAMP ASSIGNMENT
[ ] COMMAND MANAGER
[ ] DIRECT COMMUNITY SERVICES
[ ] HCSC
[ ] CHIEF, CLASSIFICATION & TREATMENT
[ ] NO ACTION REQUIRED

CLASSIFICATION REFERRAL / ADMINISTRATIVE SEGREGATION

REVIEW PERIOD: 3/13/96 TO 3/29/96 FACILITY/LIVING UNIT: CBCC/IMU

1. REFERRAL AGENT	DATE	2. MX I.D	3. NRD
K. Shanahan, CCII	3/29/96	6/26/2036	3/97

4. REVIEW OF CLASSIFICATION FOR:

[ ] INITIAL (RC)	[ ] Camp	[ ] W/R	[ ] Board
[ ] Six Month Review	[X] Ad Seg	[ ] PPR	[ ] Transfer
[ ] Other (specify) 1st Administrative Segregation Classification (16-day)			

5. NARRATIVE

REASON FOR PLACEMENT: Inmate Wright was placed on Administrative Segregation after he was identified as a possible instigator of the work stoppage which occurred on 3/4/96.

PROGRAMMING: Inmate Wright was admitted to the system on 6/16/94. He arrived at CBCC on 7/13/94. Since being placed in Segregation he has not programmed.

SERIOUS INFRACTION RECORD: There are no serious infractions to note during this review period.

MEDICAL: There are no serious medical or dental concerns to note during this review period.

MENTAL HEALTH: Mental health services have not been requested or received during this reporting period.

COMMUNITY SUPPORT: Inmate Wright states he receives support from his parents, George and Roberta Wright of Seattle. Their phone number is (206) 546-6226.

COMMUNITY RELEASE PLAN: A release plan has not been formulated at this time.

COUNSELOR COMMENTS: Inmate Wright is under SRA jurisdiction with an ERD of 4/25/2030. Community placement is required. He has legal financial obligations payable to King County Superior Court. He has a custody review score of 58 but must remain close custody per policy.

On 3/13/96 Inmate Wright was placed on Administrative Segregation after he was identified as a possible instigator of the work stoppage which occurred on 3/4/96. The investigation into this matter determined he was not involved in the work stoppage. Therefore, it is recommended he maintain close custody and be released to general population.

UNIT TEAM COMMENTS/RECOMMENDATIONS:

DATE OF MEETING: 3/29/96

STAFF PRESENT: K. Lonergan, CUS
K. Shanahan, CCII
C/O Nejira

INMATE COMMENTS: Inmate Wright stated his past shows he has not been any kind of management problem. He said he knew Sunday the work stoppage was going to happen. He was told by other kitchen workers. He said Monday was his day off and when inmates asked if he would go to work, he said he didn't have to.

COMMITTEE COMMENTS: Inmate Wright's conduct in IMU is appropriate. He has programmed his entire incarceration. He was identified as a

6 NUMBER	NAME: LAST	FIRST	MIDDLE
709976	WRIGHT,	Matthew	

CLASSIFICATION REFERRAL / ADMINISTRATIVE SEGREGATION CONTINUED

REVIEW PERIOD: 3/13/96   TO   3/29/96   FACILITY / LIVING UNIT: CBCC/IMU

possible participant in the work stoppage. The investigation into
this matter is complete. Nothing was found to show his involvement.

RECOMMENDATIONS:

1. Maintain close custody.

2. Release to CBCC general population.

Robert Doss

UNIT TEAM CHAIRPERSON   4-3-96
                                  DATE

REVIEW COMMITTEE:

Release from Ad Seg

Kathleen M Kaath Cpu

REVIEW COMMITTEE CHAIRPERSON   4-5-96
                                      DATE

SUPERINTENDENT: _Concur - to be released 4-18-96_

John P Sowle for R. C. Wright   4-6-96

SUPERINTENDENT   DATE

7. NUMBER	NAME: LAST	FIRST	MIDDLE
709976	WRIGHT,	Matthew	

DOC 5-30C CONT. (REV. 12-87)

DOCKET:
[ ] TRANSFER
[ ] COMMAND MANAGER
[ ] HCSC
[ ] CHIEF, CLASSIFICATION & TREATMENT
[ ] OVERRIDE
[ ] IMS
[ ] NO ACTION REQUIRED/FILE

REVIEW PERIOD: 2/16/96 TO 2/18/97   FACILITY/LIVING UNIT CBCC A UNIT

REFERRAL AGENT	DATE	(P)ERD	NRD	MAX ED
C. Leahy, CCIII	2/18/97	5/5/30	3/98	6/26/36

REVIEW OF CLASSIFICATION FOR:

[ ] INITIAL (RC)   [ ] Camp   [ ] W/R   [ ] Board
[X] Six Month/Annual Review [ ] Ad Seg   [ ] CPR/PPR   [ ] Transfer
[ ] HCSC   [ ] IMS   [ ] Override
[ ] Other (specify) _____   [X] No Action

NARRATIVE

PROGRAMMING: Inmate Wright was admitted to the system 3/16/94. He arrived at CBCC on 7/13/94. During this review period he has programmed in the kitchen as a kitchen worker, and has just been hired in Industries. He is not involved in any self help groups here at CBCC.

SERIOUS INFRACTION RECORD:

    7/11/96, (657), CBCC: Inmate Wright received four general
    infractions in a six month period.
    SANCTIONS: 10 DLGCT

MEDICAL: There are no serious medical or dental problems to note during this reporting period.

MENTAL HEALTH: Mental health services have not been requested or provided during this review period.

COMMUNITY SUPPORT: Inmate Wright states that he receives visits, letters, financial support and makes phone calls to family members.

COMMUNITY RELEASE PLAN: Inmate Wright intends to release to his mother Roberta Wright. Her address is 19623 14th Avenue Northwest, Seattle WA. 98177. Her phone number is 206/546-6226.

COUNSELOR COMMENTS: Inmate Wright is serving an SRA sentence with an ERD of 5/5/2030. He owes 24 months community placement upon release. He has LFO's of $449.80 on his King County charge and $100.00 on a future King County charge. Inmate Wright has a current custody review score of 59, however, due to policy he must remain close custody for the first four years of commitment. I recommend maintain close custody, retain CBCC.(MUR)

NUMBER	NAME: LAST	FIRST	MIDDLE
709976	WRIGHT,	Matthew	B.

DOC 5-30 (REV. 4/93)   Page ____ of ____

CLASSIFICATION REFERRAL CONTINUED

REVIEW PERIOD: 2/16/96 _____ TO ___ 2/18/97 ___ FACILITY/ LIVING UNIT _____ CBCC   A Unit ___

CLASSIFICATION COMMITTEE COMMENTS/RECOMMENDATIONS:

DATE OF MEETING: 2/18/97

STAFF PRESENT: CUS Schneider, CCIII C. Leahy, Sgt. Aguilar

INMATE COMMENTS: Inmate states the report is accurate and he has nothing to add.

COMMITTEE COMMENTS/RECOMMENDATIONS: This committee notes that inmate Wright has been programming satisfactorily and that he is not a management problem.

1.   Maintain close custody.
2.   Retain CBCC (MUR).

CL:pca

_____ Schneider, CUS _____   2/27/97
COMMITTEE CHAIRPERSON   DATE
REVIEW COMMITTEE:

concur

_____ N Cnl _____   3-3-97
REVIEW COMMITTEE CHAIRPERSON   DATE
SUPERINTENDENT:

Concur

_____ Anderson Assoc Supt _____   3/4/97
SUPERINTENDENT   DATE

6. NUMBER	NAME: LAST	FIRST	MIDDLE
709976	WRIGHT,	Matthew	B.

DOC 5-30A CONT (REV. 12/87)

DEPARTMENT OF CORRECTIONS	RECEIVED	REQUESTED HEADQUARTERS ACTION

DEPARTMENT OF CORRECTIONS

CLASSIFICATION REFERRAL

RECEIVED

MAR 2 5 1998

CBCC Records Office

[ ] NO ACTION REQUIRED/FILE
[ ] WORK RELEASE REFERRAL
TO: _____
FACILITY

REQUESTED HEADQUARTERS ACTION

[ ] HCSC
[ ] TRANSFER
[ ] OVERRIDE
[ ] OOS TRANSFER
[ ] DOP - IMS (ASSIGN, RETAIN, RELEASE)
[ ] ICOMMAND MANAGER

REVIEW PERIOD: __2/18/97__ TO __3/17/98__   FACILITY/ LIVING UNIT ___CBCC / A Unit___

REFERRAL AGENT	DATE	(P)ERD	NRD	MAX ED
C. Leahy CCIII	3/17/98	5/5/30	3/99	6/26/36

REVIEW OF CLASSIFICATION FOR:

[ ] INITIAL (RC)   [ ] Camp   [ ] W / R   [ ] Board
[X] Six Month/Annual Review [ ] Ad Seg   [ ] CPR/PPR   [X] Transfer
[ ] HCSC   [ ] IMS   [X] Override
[ ] Other (specify) _____ [ ] No Action

NARRATIVE

PROGRAMMING: Inmate Wright was admitted to the system on 3/16/94. He arrived at CBCC 7/13/94. During this review period he has been programming in education taking computer classes. He completed Anger Management classes in January 1998.

SERIOUS INFRACTION RECORD:

9/2/97, (555,600), CBCC: During a random cell search of Wright's cell, officers found six pair of rubber gloves in the battery compartment of his radio. The seal had been tampered with.
SANCTION: 10 DCC, 90 days loss of radio

MEDICAL: There are no medical or dental problems to note during this reporting period.

MENTAL HEALTH: Mental health services have not been requested or provided during this review period.

COMMUNITY SUPPORT: Inmate Wright states that he receives visits, letters, financial support and makes phone calls to his family most of whom live in Seattle.

COMMUNITY RELEASE PLAN: Inmate Wright intends to release to his mother Roberta Wright at 19623 14th Ave. NW Seattle WA 98177; phone 206/546-6226.

COUNSELOR COMMENTS: Inmate Wright is serving an SRA sentence with an ERD of 5/5/2030. He owes 24 months community placement upon release. He has LFO's in the amount of $549.80 payable to King County Superior Court. Inmate Wright has a current custody review score of 59, however, due to policy he cannot be promoted past medium custody at this time. Inmate Wright requests a transfer to WSR to be closer to his family. His family visits weekly and this has been confirmed with the visiting sergeant. I recommend promote to medium custody, transfer to WSR. (MUR)

NUMBER	NAME: LAST	FIRST	MIDDLE
709976	WRIGHT,	Matthew	B.

DOC 5-30 (REV 4/87) DOP

CLASSIFICATION COMMITTEE COMMENTS/RECOMMEN

DATE OF MEETING: 3/17/98

STAFF PRESENT: CUS Schneider, CCIII C. Leahy, Sgt. Trump

INMATE COMMENTS: Inmate stated the report was accurate and he ha add.

COMMITTEE COMMENTS/RECOMMENDATIONS: During this review p Wright has not been considered a management problem. He has maintai programming requirements and has received excellent reports from his wo

1.   Promote to medium custody. (MUR)
2.   Transfer to WSR.

CL/pca

(signature) Schneider, CUS
COMMITTEE CHAIRPERSON
REVIEW COMMITTEE:

Concur

(signature) Kathleen McKook, CPM   3-
REVIEW COMMITTEE CHAIRPERSON
SUPERINTENDENT:

Concur

(signature)
SUPERINTENDENT

709976   WRIGHT,   Matthew   B.

WRIGHT, MATTHEW #709 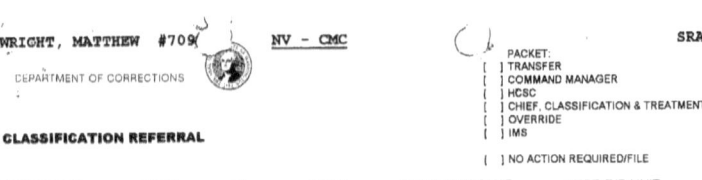 NV - CMC | SRA

DEPARTMENT OF CORRECTIONS

PACKET:
[ ] TRANSFER
[ ] COMMAND MANAGER
[ ] HCSC
[ ] CHIEF, CLASSIFICATION & TREATMENT
[ ] OVERRIDE
[ ] IMS

[ ] NO ACTION REQUIRED/FILE

CLASSIFICATION REFERRAL

REVIEW PERIOD:	2/1/98	TO	3/9/99	FACILITY/LIVING UNIT	WSR B/B UNIT

REFERRAL AGENT: CRAIG YOST, CC3/sam	DATE 3/9/99	(P)ERD. 5/5/30	NRD. 3/00	MAX ED. 6/26/36

REVIEW OF CLASSIFICATION FOR:

[ ] INITIAL (RC)	[ ] Camp	[ ] W/R	[ ] Board
[ ] Six Month	[ ] Ad Seg	[ ] CPR / PPR	[ ] Transfer
[ ] HCSC	[ ] IMS	[ ] Override	[ ] No Action
[X] Other (specify)	ANNUAL REVIEW		

NARRATIVE

PROGRAMMING: Mr. Wright arrived at WSR on 7/20/98, from CBCC. He has worked in the IK, laundry, and has been working at Compuchair (Class II industry) since 2/25/99. He is not enrolled in school.

SERIOUS INFRACTIONS: Mr. Wright has remained infraction free since 9/2/97.

MEDICAL: No medical or dental problems reported.

MENTAL HEALTH: Mr. Wright has neither requested nor required services from Mental Health staff during this review period.

COMMUNITY SUPPORT: Mr. Wright is 25 years of age, single, and has no children. He is from the Seattle area, where his parents and sister reside. He receives regular visits during the week, and participates in Extended Family Visits with family members.

COMMUNITY RELEASE PLAN: Mr. Wright is an SRA case with community placement upon release.

PROGRAM RECOMMENDATIONS:

1. **ED/VOC**: Mr. Wright received his GED at CBCC.

2. **CHEMICAL DEPENDENCY**: A SASSI has yet to be completed.

3. **STRESS/ANGER MANAGEMENT**: Recommended due to the committing offense when closer to release date.

COUNSELOR COMMENTS: Mr. Wright has medium custody per policy (MUR 1st). He was recently hired at Compuchair (Class I industry), and has a considerable amount of time until release. His primary goal at this point is to try to remain at WSR as a medium custody inmate in order to stay close to his family. He is to be commended for his programming and conduct during this review period.

UNIT TEAM COMMENTS/RECOMMENDATIONS: Mr. Wright is appearing before the Unit Team on this date for an Annual Review. He has medium custody per policy (MUR 1st). He maintains full-time programming and has been infraction free during this review period.

NUMBER	NAME LAST	FIRST	MIDDLE
#709976	WRIGHT	MATTHEW	

WRIGHT, MATTHEW #709

DEPARTMENT OF CORRECTIONS

CLASSIFICATION REFERRAL, continued

REVIEW PERIOD: 2/1/98 TO 3/9/99   FACILITY/LIVING UNIT   WSR B/B UNIT

UNIT TEAM RECOMMENDS:

1. Custody remains medium (MUR 1st) per policy.
2. Commend conduct

PROGRAM RECOMMENDATIONS:

1. Continue participation in Compuchair assignment.

INMATE COMMENTS: None. Inmate was reviewed in absentia at his own request.

COMMITTEE MEMBERS: Bill Woodley, CUS; Craig Yost, CC3; Bob Pittsenbarger, CC2; and Sgt. Jennings.

CUS Bill Wood

Chairperson/Date   UNIT TEAM DATE: 3/17/99

Review Committee Recommendations/Action:

Custody remains Medium.
Continue present programming.

Review Committee Chairperson/Date: P. Seeberg 4-5-99

Superintendent Recommendations/Actions:

Concur

Superintendent Signature/Date: _____ 4-5-99

NUMBER	NAME LAST	FIRST	MIDDLE
#709976	WRIGHT	MATTHEW	

DOC 5-30 (REV. 4/93)

WRIGHT, MATTHEW #709976   √ - CMC   SRA

DEPARTMENT OF CORRECTIONS

CLASSIFICATION REFERRAL

PACKET:
[ ] TRANSFER
[ ] COMMAND MANAGER
[ ] HCSC
[ ] CHIEF, CLASSIFICATION & TREATMENT
[ ] OVERRIDE
[ ] IMS

[ ] NO ACTION REQUIRED/FILE

REVIEW PERIOD:	3/10/99	TO	3/3/00	FACILITY/LIVING UNIT	MCC-WSRU B UNIT

REFERRAL AGENT:		DATE	(P)ERD:	NRD:	MAX ED:
CRAIG YOST, C/C3/ph		3/8/00	5/5/30	3/01	6/26/36

REVIEW OF CLASSIFICATION FOR:

[ ] INITIAL (RC)	[ ] Camp	[ ] W / R	[ ] Board
[X] Six Month/**Annual Review**	[ ] Ad Seg	[ ] CPR / PPR	[ ] Transfer
[ ] HCSC	[ ] IMS	[ ] Override	[ ] No Action
[ ] Other (specify)			

NARRATIVE

PROGRAMMING: Mr. Wright has been employed at CompuChair since 2/99. Most of his free time is spent visiting with his family.

SERIOUS INFRACTIONS: Mr. Wright has remained infraction free since 9/2/97.

MEDICAL: No medical or dental problems reported.

MENTAL HEALTH: Mr. Wright has neither requested nor required services from Mental Health staff during this review period.

COMMUNITY SUPPORT: Mr. Wright is 26 years of age, single, and has no children. He is from the Seattle area, where his parents and sister reside. He receives regular visits during the week, and participates in Extended Family Visits with family members.

COMMUNITY RELEASE PLAN: Mr. Wright is an SRA case with community placement upon release.

OFFENDER ACCOUNTABILITY PLAN:

1. ED/VOC: Mr. Wright received his GED at CBCC.

2. CHEMICAL DEPENDENCY: A SASSI has yet to be completed.

3. STRESS/ANGER MANAGEMENT: Recommended due to the committing offense when closer to release date.

4. VICTIM AWARENESS: Recommended due to the committing offense when closer to release date.

5. LSI-R: Low/moderate risk/needs.

COUNSELOR COMMENTS: Mr. Wright has medium custody per policy (MUR 1st). He was recently hired at Compuchair (Class I industry), and has a considerable amount of time until release. His primary goal at this point is to try to remain at WSR as a medium custody inmate in order to stay close to his family. He is to be commended for his programming and conduct during this review period.

UNIT TEAM COMMENTS/RECOMMENDATIONS: Mr. Wright is appearing before the Unit Team on this date for an Annual Review. He has medium custody per policy (MUR 1st). He maintains full-time programming and has been infraction free during this review period.

UNIT TEAM RECOMMENDS:

1. Custody remains medium per policy, (MUR 1st).
2. Commend programming and conduct.

PROGRAM RECOMMENDATIONS:
None noted.

NUMBER	NAME LAST	FIRST	MIDDLE
#709976	WRIGHT	MATTHEW	

WRIGHT, MATTHEW #709976

CLASSIFICATION REFERRAL, continued

REVIEW PERIOD: __3/9/00__ TO __3/3/00__ FACILITY/LIVING UNIT __MCC-WSRU B UNIT__

INMATE COMMENTS: Mr. Wright stated that he was doing alright working at his Class I job at CompuChair and wished to remain at WSR.

COMMITTEE MEMBERS: Craig Yost, CC3; Steven Sundberg, CC2; Sgt. Ted Bucher.

Yost 4/13/00
Chairperson/Date   UNIT TEAM DATE: 3/29/00

Review Committee Recommendations/Action: _dp_

    Custody remains Medium.
    Continue present programming.

Review Committee Chairperson/Date: _P. Leeberg 4-27-00_

Superintendent Recommendations/Actions: _Concur_

Superintendent Signature/Date: _____ _5-1-00_

NUMBER	NAME LAST	FIRST	MIDDLE
#709976	WRIGHT	MATTHEW	

DOC 5-30 (REV. 4/93)

DEPARTMENT OF CORRECTIONS

PACKET:
[   ] TRANSFER
[   ] COMMAND MANAGER
[   ] HCSC
[   ] CHIEF, CLASSIFICATION &
        TREATMENT
[   ] OVERRIDE
[   ] IMS

[   ] NO ACTION REQUIRED/FILE

CLASSIFICATION REFERRAL

REVIEW PERIOD:	3/04/00	TO	2/20/01	FACILITY/LIVING UNIT	MCC-WSRU B UNIT

REFERRAL AGENT:		DATE	(P)ERD:	NRD:	MAX ED:
CRAIG YOST, CC3/ph		3/05/01	5/5/30	3/02	6/26/36

REVIEW OF CLASSIFICATION FOR:

[ ] INITIAL (RC)	[ ] Camp	[ ] W / R	[ ] Board
[X] Six Month/**Annual Review**	[ ] Ad Seg	[ ] CPR / PPR	[ ] Transfer
[ ] HCSC	[ ] IMS	[ ] Override	[ ] No Action
[ ] Other (specify)			

NARRATIVE

PROGRAMMING: Mr. Wright has been employed at CompuChair since 2/99. Most of his free time is spent visiting with his family.

SERIOUS INFRACTIONS:

1/05/01 WAC # 505 (FIGHTING): Wright was observed arguing with inmate Stephens # 728283 in the Field House. They were then observed exchanging blows to the face and head. Assistance was called to control the situation and they were given orders to stop fighting and back away. Both inmates refused to comply and staff were forced to intervene to separate the inmates. Inmate Stephens was escorted to the 3rd Floor Hospital. SANCTION: 15 days SDS, credit for 7 days served, 8 days suspended for 90 days provided no further serious infractions during that time span.

MEDICAL: No medical or dental problems reported.

MENTAL HEALTH: Mr. Wright has neither requested nor required services from Mental Health staff during this review period.

COMMUNITY SUPPORT: Mr. Wright is 27 years of age, single, and has no children. He is from the Seattle area, where his parents and sister reside. He receives regular visits during the week, and participates in Extended Family Visits with family members.

COMMUNITY RELEASE PLAN: Mr. Wright is an SRA case with community placement upon release. He owes legal financial obligations of $55.25 on Cause A and Cause B is paid off.

OFFENDER ACCOUNTABILITY PLAN:

1. **ED/VOC**: Mr. Wright received his GED at CBCC.

2. **CHEMICAL DEPENDENCY**: A SASSI has yet to be completed.

3. **STRESS/ANGER MANAGEMENT**: Recommended due to the committing offense when closer to release date.

4. **VICTIM AWARENESS**: Recommended due to the committing offense when closer to release date.

5. **LSI-R**: Low/moderate risk/needs.

COUNSELOR COMMENTS: Mr. Wright has medium custody per policy (MUR 1st). He continues to work at CompuChair (Class I industry). As a result of the fight, he was allowed to work pending no infractions. His primary goal at this point is to try to remain at WSR as a medium custody inmate in order to stay close to his family. He is to be commended for his programming but encouraged to improve his conduct record.

UNIT TEAM COMMENTS/RECOMMENDATIONS: Mr. Wright is appearing before the Unit Team on this date for an Annual Review. He has medium custody per policy (MUR 1st). He maintains full-time programming with a Class I Industry and has received the above listed infraction this review period. His job is conditional upon receiving no further serious infractions.

NUMBER	NAME LAST	FIRST	MIDDLE
#709976	WRIGHT	MATTHEW	

DEPARTMENT OF CORRECTIONS

CLASSIFICATION REFERRAL, continued

REVIEW PERIOD: __3/04/00__ TO __2/20/01__ FACILITY/LIVING UNIT __MCC-WSRU B UNIT__

UNIT TEAM RECOMMENDS:

1. Custody remains medium per policy, (MUR 1st).
2. Improve conduct.

OFFENDER ACCOUNTABILITY PLANS:

1. Continue participation in CompuChair assignment.

INMATE COMMENTS: Mr. Wright stated that his supervisor told him he had a CIN hold.

COMMITTEE MEMBERS: Bill Woodley, CUS; Craig Yost, CC3; Steven Sundberg, CC2; Sgt. Wardlaw.

_____ UNIT TEAM DATE: 3/14/01
Chairperson/Date

Review Committee Recommendations/Action:

Custody remains medium.
Continue present program.

Review Committee Chairperson/Date: _P. Lieberg 4-3-01_

Superintendent Recommendations/Actions: Concur

Superintendent Signature/Date: _____ 4-4-01

NUMBER	NAME LAST	FIRST	MIDDLE
#709976	WRIGHT	MATTHEW	

DOC 1 38 (REV. 4/93)

WRICHT, MATTHEW #70.

SRA

DEPARTMENT OF CORRECTIONS

CLASSIFICATION REFERRAL

PACKET:
[ ] TRANSFER
[ ] COMMAND MANAGER
[ ] HCSC
[ ] CHIEF, CLASSIFICATION & TREATMENT
[ ] OVERRIDE
[ ] IMS

[ ] NO ACTION REQUIRED/FILE

REVIEW PERIOD:	2/21/01	TO	3/7/02	FACILITY/LIVING UNIT	MCC/WSRU B-UNIT

REFERRAL AGENT: CRAIG YOST, CC3/law		DATE 3/14/02	(P)ERD: 5/5/30	NRD: 3/03	MAX ED: 6/26/36

REVIEW OF CLASSIFICATION FOR:

[ ] INITIAL (RC) [ ] Camp [ ] W/R [ ] Board
[X] Annual Review [ ] Ad Seg [ ] CPR/PPR [ ] Transfer
[ ] HCSC [ ] IMS [ ] Override [ ] No Action
[ ] Other (specify)

NARRATIVE

PROGRAMMING: Mr. Wright has been employed at CompuChair since 2/99. Most of his free time is spent visiting with his family.

SERIOUS INFRACTIONS: None during this review period.

MEDICAL: No medical or dental problems reported.

MENTAL HEALTH: Mr. Wright has neither requested nor required services from Mental Health staff during this review period.

COMMUNITY SUPPORT: Mr. Wright is 28 years of age, single, and has no children. He is from the Seattle area, where his parents and sister reside. He receives regular visits during the week, and participates in Extended Family Visits with family members.

COMMUNITY RELEASE PLAN: Mr. Wright is an SRA case with community placement upon release. He owes legal financial obligations of $55.25 on Cause A and Cause B is paid off.

OFFENDER ACCOUNTABILITY PLAN:

1. **ED/VOC**: Mr. Wright received his GED at CBCC.

2. **CHEMICAL DEPENDENCY**: A SASSI has yet to be completed.

3. **STRESS/ANGER MANAGEMENT**: Recommended due to the committing offense when closer to release date.

4. **VICTIM AWARENESS**: Recommended due to the committing offense when closer to release date.

5. **LSI-R**: Low/moderate risk/needs.

COUNSELOR COMMENTS: Mr. Wright has medium custody per policy (MUR 1st). He continues to work at CompuChair (Class I industry). Mr. Wright continues to work full time and remain infraction free. He is to be commended for his program and behavior efforts during this review period.

NUMBER	NAME LAST	FIRST	MIDDLE
#709976	WRIGHT	MATTHEW	

WRIGHT, MATTHEW #70

DEPARTMENT OF CORRECTIONS

CLASSIFICATION REFERRAL, continued

REVIEW PERIOD: 2/21/01 TO 3/7/02   FACILITY/LIVING UNIT   **MCC/WSRU B-UNIT**

UNIT TEAM COMMENTS/RECOMMENDATIONS: Mr. Wright has medium custody per policy, continues working at CompuChair and remains infraction free.

UNIT TEAM RECOMMENDATIONS:
1. Custody remains medium (MUR 1st).
2. Continue CIN hold until 1/24/05.
3. Commend conduct.

OFFENDER ACCOUNTABILITY PLAN
1. Continue participation in CompuChair assignment.

INMATE COMMENTS: None.

COMMITTEE MEMBERS: Bill Woodley, CUS; Craig Yost, CC3; Steve Sundberg, CC2; Sgt. Dave Johnson

Chairperson/Date _Bill Woodle_   Unit Team Date: 3/27/02
Review Committee Recommendations/Action

Custody remains Medium.
Continue present programming.

Review Committee Chairperson/Date: _P. Leeberg_   4-5-02
Superintendent Recommendations/Actions: _Concur_

Superintendent Signature/Date: _____ 4-5-02

NUMBER	NAME LAST	FIRST	MIDDLE
#709976	**WRIGHT**	**MATTHEW**	

DOC 5-30 (REV. 4/93)

CLASSIFICATION REFERRAL

STATE OF WASHINGTON
DEPARTMENT OF CORRECTIONS

REQUESTED DOC HQ ACTION
[ ] Command Manager [ ] Direct Community Services	[ ] Electronic ____ Camp ____ PR
[ ] HCSC/Chief, Class & Treatment	[ ] IMS (Assign, Retain, Release)
[ ] OOS Transfer [ ] Override [ ] Transfer	[ ] WR, Referral to _____
[X] HQ File, No Action Required	

REVIEW PERIOD: __9-02__ TO: __9-02__ FACILITY/LIVING UNIT: __WSP/MSC/BAR__

| REFERRAL AGENT: | DATE: | (P) ERD: | NRD: | MAX EX: |
| D. MCKINNEY, CCII D. ...9-24-02 | 9-4-02 | 5-5-30 | 9-4-03 | 6-26-36 |

REVIEW OR CLASSIFICATION FOR:
[ ] INITIAL (RC)	[X] SIX MONTH REVIEW	[ ] ANNUAL REVIEW	[ ] HCSC
[ ] CAMP	[ ] AD SEG	[ ] IMS [ ] W/R	[ ] CPR/PPR
[ ] OVERRIDE	[ ] BOARD	[ ] TRANSFER [ ] NO ACTION	[ ] OTHER (SPECIFY)

NARRATIVE:

CUSTODY: Wright is currently assigned to Medium Custody on a MUR Override. Wright's CRS is 61. One programming point was deducted due to negative behavior in May, 2002. Wright was ultimately transferred from MCC due to disruptive behavior during a facility lockdown situation. He is not eligible for promotion to Minimum Custody until he's within 48-months of ERD. My recommendation is to retain Medium Custody, MUR.

PLACEMENT: Wright was transferred from E01 to E02 on 8-23-02. My recommendation is to retain placement at WSP/MSC.

PROGRAMS:
Basic Skills: Inmate Wright earned his GED while housed at CBCC.

Work: Wright is currently waiting to be assigned to Custodial Services, Maintenance, or Groundskeeper. He has prior Correctional Industries experience. Wright's previous employer rated his performance as exceptional.

Offender Change Programs: Referrals for Achieving Your Potential, Critical Thinking, and Victim Awareness were made on 9-4-02. He will not be approved for OCI classes until 5-5-28.

Vocational Programs: No vocational classes have been completed during this review period. Wright wishes to enroll in the Custodial Services Program.

ADDITIONAL EXPECTATIONS: Inmate Wright is expected to follow all DOC rules while housed at WSP/MSC. He is expected to participate in a full-time program while housed at WSP/MSC.
DM:js 9-9-02
Reason past MFED: 000 Reason past PRE-REL: 999 Reason past WTR: 000 Reason past REL: 000.

FACILITY RISK MANAGEMENT TEAM 09/17/02: CHM W. Ponti; CC3 L. Sutton; CC2 S. Jacobson; CC2 D. McKinney; Sgt. M. Johnson.

INMATE COMMENTS: None.

FRMT COMMENTS & ACTIONS: Current custody is Medium, CRS 61, P/ERD 5-5-30, LSI-R Score 15.
1) Retain on Medium Custody. Assign MUR Override. Retain at E02.
2) Targeting promotion to lower custody not recommended due to policy.
3) Maintain programming as outlined in this Facility Plan.
4) Validate Earned Time for this Review Period.
5) Schedule next Regular Review on 9-4-03.

FRMT CHAIRPERSON: _W. J. Ponti_   DATE: _9/25/02_

REVIEW COMMITTEE COMMENTS & RECOMMENDATIONS:
Concur

SIGNATURE OF REVIEW COMMITTEE MEMBERS: _S. Conrad L. Sutton H. _____   DATE: _9/27/02_

SUPERINTENDENT/DESIGNEE: _____   DATE: _9-30-02_

| NUMBER | NAME: LAST | FIRST | MIDDLE |
| 709976 | WRIGHT, | Matthew | B. |

DOC 300.380   DOC 320.180   DOC 320.200
DOC 320.250   DOC 350.100   DOC 350.270
DOC 350.275

```
                        STATE OF WASHINGTON
                     DEPARTMENT OF CORRECTIONS
                          CUSTODY REVIEW

     09/04/2002           COUNSELORS NAME: 1144 MCKINNEY, DAVID A
-----------------------------------------------------------------------
| I. CURRENT CUSTODY DESIGNATION:                        *            |
|    ---------------------------                         *            |
|      MINIMUM:                                          *            |
|         COMMUNITY = . 15                               *            |
|         INSTITUTION = 10                               *            |
|      MEDIUM = ...... 5                                 *            |
|      CLOSE  = ...... 2                                 *            |
|      MAXIMUM = ..... 0                                 *   SCORE = 5 |
-----------------------------------------------------------------------
| II. INFRACTION BEHAVIOR:                               *            |
|     -------------------                                *            |
|        ANY  A INFRACTION (PAST 2 YRS) -20             *            |
|        EACH B INFRACTION (PAST 6 MOS) -10   NONE = 20  *            |
|        EACH C INFRACTION (PAST 6 MOS) -5   DEDUCT. = 0 *            |
|                                            --          *            |
|          TOTAL DEDUCTIONS (UP TO -20) - 0   TOTAL = 20 *            |
|                                                        *            |
|        IF POINTS = 0, STOP. HAS THIS INMATE BEEN DEMOTED *          |
|        IN PREVIOUS REVIEWS FOR THESE SAME INFRACTIONS?  *  Y OR N:  |
|        YES - CONTINUE; NO - CUSTODY MUST DEMOTE AT LEAST *          |
|        ONE STEP. MAX PLACEMENT REQUIRES DIRECTORS APPROVAL * SCORE = 20 |
-----------------------------------------------------------------------
|III. PROGRAM BEHAVIOR:                                  *            |
|     ----------------                                   *            |
|        NUMBER OF MONTHS OFFENDER PROGRAMMED.           *            |
|           6 MOS. REVIEW  __ X 2 = __                   *            |
|           ANNUAL REVIEW  11 X 1 = 11                   *  SCORE = 11 |
-----------------------------------------------------------------------
| IV. DETAINERS:                                         *            |
|     ---------                                          *            |
|        NONE = . 10                                     *            |
|        INS = .. 8                                      *            |
|        FELONY = 0                                      *  SCORE = 10 |
-----------------------------------------------------------------------
| V. ESCAPE HISTORY:                                     *            |
|    --------------                                      *            |
|        NONE = ..................... 15                 *            |
|        2 YRS. 1 DAY THROUGH 10 YRS. = 10              *            |
|        WITHIN PAST 2 YEARS = ........ 0               *  SCORE = 15 |
-----------------------------------------------------------------------
|    CUSTODY:                                            *  TOTAL     |
|    -------                                             *  SCORE = 61 |
|      0 - 39 = CLO    40 - 55 = MED    56 + = MIN       *            |
|                                                        *  CUSTODY = MIN |
-----------------------------------------------------------------------
| OVERRIDE/REASON:      | ASSIGNED CUSTODY: med                        |
|    ___mur_____      | BY: EN85 _____  9 27 02  |
|                       | FACILITY ADMINISTRATOR/DOOP DIRECTOR   DATE  |
-----------------------------------------------------------------------
|                                                                     |
|      DOC NUMBER: 709976       NAME: MATTHEW B. WRIGHT               |
-----------------------------------------------------------------------
```

CLASSIFICATION REFERRAL

STATE OF WASHINGTON
DEPARTMENT OF CORRECTIONS

REQUESTED DOC HQ ACTION

[   ] Command Manager   [   ] Direct Community Services   [   ] Electronic ____ Camp
[   ] HCSC/Chief, Class & Treatment   [   ] IMS (Assign, Retain, Release,
[   ] OOB Transfer   [   ] Override   [   ] Transfer   [   ] WR, Referral to ____
[X] HQ File, No Action Required

REVIEW PERIOD: 09-04-02	To: 01-29-03	FACILITY/LIVING UNIT:	WSP/MSC/BAR		
REFERRAL AGENT: C. Meyer, CC2 *Cm*	DATE: 01-29-03	P) ERD: 05-05-30	NRD: 01-04	MAX EX: 06-26-36	

REVIEW OF CLASSIFICATION FOR:

[ ] INITIAL (RC)	[X] SIX MONTH REVIEW	[ ] ANNUAL REVIEW		[ ] HCSC
[ ] CAMP	[ ] AD SEG	[ ] IMS	[ ] W/R	[ ] CPR/PPR
[ ] OVERRIDE	[ ] BOARD	[ ] TRANSFER	[ ] NO ACTION	[ ] OTHER (SPECIFY)

NARRATIVE:

CUSTODY: Wright has Medium Custody, MUR Override. CRS is 62. Retain Medium Custody, transfer to MCC per policy 530.150 – Hardship Transfers. Wright requested TRCC, however, he has a separatee at TRCC. Wright has been infraction free since 01-05-01.

PLACEMENT: Wright was received from WSP/MI on 08-32-02. Transfer to MCC per hardship policy.

PROGRAMS:

Basic Skills: Wright earned his GED in 1994.

Work: Wright is currently employed as a custodian.

Offender Change Programs: Wright has been approved for Achieving Your Potential, Critical Thinking, and Victim Awareness.

Vocational Programs: Wright has completed Custodial Services.

ADDITIONAL EXPECTATIONS: Wright is expected to remain infraction free and continue to program while housed at WSP/MSC. CM:js 01-30-03

Reason past MFED: 000 Reason past PRE-REL: 000 Reason past WTR: 000 Reason past REL: 000.

FACILITY RISK MANAGEMENT TEAM 2-4-03: W. Ponti, CHM; S. Jacobson, CCIII; C. Spencer, CCIII; J. Denny, CCII; L. Schulke, CCII; V. Gaines, CCII; C. Meyer, CCII

INMATE COMMENTS: None.

FRMT COMMENTS & ACTIONS: Committee supports hardship transfer. Inmate requests MICC to be closer to his family. Current Custody - Medium (MUR); CRS 62; P/ERD 5-5-30; LSI-R Score 22

1. Retain Medium Custody; MUR Override.
2. Targeting promotion to lower custody not recommended due to ERD.
3. Transfer to MICC/Medium.
4. Maintain programming as outlined in this Facility Plan.

FRMT CHAIRPERSON: _W. Ponti_   DATE: 2/7/03

REVIEW COMMITTEE COMMENTS & RECOMMENDATIONS:

Retain Medium Custody at WSP/MSC
Deny request for transfer to MICC as policy restricts
inmate placement due to his offense.
(MUR override)

SIGNATURE OF REVIEW COMMITTEE MEMBERS _Ray Jensen S. Conrad H. Bigham_   DATE: 2-7-03

SUPERINTENDENT/DESIGNEE: DATE: 2-7-03

NUMBER	NAME: LAST	FIRST	MIDDLE
709976	WRIGHT,	Matthew	B.

DOC 300.380   DOC 320.180   DOC 320.200
DOC 320.250   DOC 350.100   DOC 350.270
DOC 350.275

```
                    STATE OF WASHINGTON
                 DEPARTMENT OF CORRECTIONS
                      CUSTODY REVIEW

    01/29/2003          COUNSELORS NAME: 1144 MEYER, CINDY
-----------------------------------------------------------------------
| I. CURRENT CUSTODY DESIGNATION:                        *  i         |
|    ---------------------------                         *            |
|      MINIMUM:                                          *.           |
|         COMMUNITY = . 15                               *            |
|         INSTITUTION = 10                               *            |
|      MEDIUM = ...... 5                                 *            |
|      CLOSE  = ...... 2                                 *            |
|      MAXIMUM = ..... 0                                 *  SCORE =  5 |
-----------------------------------------------------------------------
| II. INFRACTION BEHAVIOR:                               *            |
|     -------------------                                *            |
|      ANY  A INFRACTION (PAST 2 YRS) -20               *            |
|      EACH B INFRACTION (PAST 6 MOS) -10    NONE = 20  *            |
|      EACH C INFRACTION (PAST 6 MOS)  -5  DEDUCT. =  0 *            |
|                                            --         *            |
|        TOTAL DEDUCTIONS (UP TO -20) - 0    TOTAL = 20 *            |
|                                                       *            |
|      IF POINTS = 0, STOP. HAS THIS INMATE BEEN DEMOTED *           |
|      IN PREVIOUS REVIEWS FOR THESE SAME INFRACTIONS?   * Y OR N:    |
|      YES - CONTINUE; NO - CUSTODY MUST DEMOTE AT LEAST *            |
|      ONE STEP. MAX PLACEMENT REQUIRES DIRECTORS APPROVAL * SCORE = 20 |
-----------------------------------------------------------------------
|III. PROGRAM BEHAVIOR:                                  *            |
|     ---------------                                    *            |
|      NUMBER OF MONTHS OFFENDER PROGRAMMED.             *            |
|         6 MOS. REVIEW __ X 2 = __                      *            |
|         ANNUAL REVIEW  12 X 1 = 12                     * SCORE = 12 |
-----------------------------------------------------------------------
| IV. DETAINERS:                                         *            |
|     ---------                                          *            |
|         NONE = . 10                                    *            |
|         INS = .. 8                                     *            |
|         FELONY =  0                                    * SCORE = 10 |
-----------------------------------------------------------------------
| V. ESCAPE HISTORY:                                     *            |
|    --------------                                      *            |
|         NONE = ..................... 15               *            |
|         2 YRS. 1 DAY THROUGH 10 YRS. = 10             *            |
|         WITHIN PAST 2 YEARS = ........ 0             * SCORE = 15 |
-----------------------------------------------------------------------
|    CUSTODY:                                            * TOTAL      |
|    -------                                             * SCORE = 62 |
|      0 - 39 = CLO    40 - 55 = MED    56 + = MIN      *            |
|                                                       * CUSTODY = MIN|
-----------------------------------------------------------------------
| OVERRIDE/REASON:      | ASSIGNED CUSTODY: MW                        |
|    MUK                | BY: ONBB _____  2/7/03           |
|                       | FACILITY ADMINISTRATOR/DOOP DIRECTOR  DATE  |
-----------------------------------------------------------------------
|                                                                     |
|    DOC NUMBER: 709976       NAME: MATTHEW B. WRIGHT                 |
|                                                                     |
-----------------------------------------------------------------------
```

STATE OF WASHINGTON
DEPARTMENT OF CORRECTIONS

CLASSIFICATION APPEAL   MICC

REQUESTED DOC HQ ACTION

[ ] Command Manager	[ ] Direct Community Services	[ ] Electronic ____ Camp ____ PR
[ ] HCSC/Chief, Class & Treatment		[ ] IMS (Assign, Retain, Release)
[ ] OOS Transfer	[ ] Override [ ] Transfer	[ ] WR, Referral to ____
[X] HQ File, No Action Required		

REVIEW PERIOD: __01-29-03__ To: __03-27-03__   FACILITY/LIVING UNIT: __WSP/MSC/BAR__

REFERRAL AGENT:	DATE:	P/ERD:	NRD:	MAX EX:
C. MEYER, CC2	03-27-03	05-05-30	03-04	06-26-36

REVIEW OF CLASSIFICATION FOR:

[ ] INITIAL (RC)	[X] SIX MONTH REVIEW	[ ] ANNUAL REVIEW	[ ] HCSC
[ ] CAMP	[ ] AD SEG	[ ] IMS [ ] W/R	[ ] CPR/PPR
[ ] OVERRIDE	[ ] BOARD	[ ] TRANSFER [ ] NO ACTION	[ ] OTHER (SPECIFY)

NARRATIVE:

CUSTODY: Wright has Medium Custody, CRS is 62. Promote to MI3 and transfer to MICC per policy 530.150 – Hardship Transfers. Wright has been infraction free since 01-05-01.

PLACEMENT: Wright was received from WSP/MI on 08-23-02. Transfer to MICC per Hardship Policy.

PROGRAMS:
Basic Skills: Wright earned his GED in 1994.

Work: Wright is currently employed as a custodian.

Offender Change Programs: Wright has been approved for Achieving Your Potential, Critical Thinking and Victim Awareness.

Vocational Programs: Wright has completed Custodial Services.

ADDITIONAL EXPECTATIONS: Wright is expected to remain infraction free and continue to program while housed at WSP/MSC.

CJM:js 03-28-03

Reason past MFED: 000 Reason past PRE-REL: 000 Reason past WTR: 000 Reason past REL: 000.

FACILITY RISK MANAGEMENT TEAM 04/01/03: CHM Ponti; CC3 Jacobson; CC3 Spencer; CC2 Denny; CC2 Schulke; CC2 Gaines; CC2 Meyer; Sgt. Johnson.

INMATE COMMENTS: None.

FRMT COMMENTS & ACTIONS: Current custody is Medium, CRS 62, P/ERD 05-05-30, LSI-R Score 22.
1) Promote from Medium to MI3 Custody. Assignment Override
2) Targeting promotion to lower custody not recommended due to ERD.
3) Transfer to MICC per hardship policy, Priority 3M.
4) Maintain programming as outlined in this Facility Plan.

FRMT CHAIRPERSON: _____   DATE: 4/1/03

REVIEW COMMITTEE COMMENTS & RECOMMENDATIONS:

Concur

SIGNATURE OF REVIEW COMMITTEE MEMBERS _____ Lt. Bynum ____   DATE: 4-4-03

SUPERINTENDENT/DESIGNEE: _____   DATE: 04-7-03

NUMBER	NAME: LAST	FIRST	MIDDLE
709976	WRIGHT,	Matthew	B.

DOC 20-030 (Rev. 2/5/02) POL

DOC 300.380   DOC 320.180   DOC 320.200
DOC 320.250   DOC 350.100   DOC 350.270
DOC 350.275

Disciplinary Sanction Table

(Major Infractions)

Category A-20 classification points

Infraction

501	Committing homicide
502	Aggravated assault on another offender
507	Committing an act that would constitute a felony and that is not otherwise included in these rules
511	Aggravated assault on a visitor or community member
521	Taking or holding any person hostage
550	Escape
601	Possession, manufacture, or introduction of an explosive device or any ammunition, or any components of an explosive device or ammunition
602	Possession, manufacture, or introduction of any gun, firearm, weapon, sharpened instrument, knife, or poison or any component thereof
603	Possession, introduction, use, or transfer of any narcotic, controlled substance, illegal drug, unauthorized drug, mind altering, substance, or drug paraphernalia
604	Aggravated assault on a staff member
611	Sexual assault on a staff member
612	Attempted sexual assault on a staff member
613	Abusive sexual contact with staff
635	Sexual assault on another offender
636	Attempted sexual assault on another offender

637	Abusive sexual contact with another offender
650	Rioting
651	Inciting others to riot

Category B-10 classification points
LEVEL 1

Infraction

504	Engaging in sexual acts with others within the facility with the exception of approved conjugal visits
553	Setting a fire
560	Unauthorized possession of items or materials likely to be used in an escape attempt
633	Assault on another offender
704	Assault on a staff member
711	Assault on a visitor or community member
744	Making a bomb threat

Category B-10 classification points
LEVEL 2

Infraction

505	Fighting with any person
556	Refusing to submit or cooperate in a search when ordered to do so by a staff member
607	Refusing to submit to a urinalysis and/or failure to provide a urine sample when ordered to do so by a staff member within the allotted time frame
608	Refusing or failure to submit to a breathalyzer or other sobriety test when ordered to do so by a staff member
609	Refusing or failure to submit to testing required by policy, statute, or court order, such as DNA blood tests, when ordered to do so by a staff member

652	Engaging in or inciting a group demonstration
655	Making intoxicants, alcohol, controlled substances, narcotics, or possession of ingredients, equipment, items, formulas, or instructions that are used in making intoxicants, alcohol, controlled substances, or narcotics
682	Engaging in or inciting an organized work stoppage
707	Possession, introduction, or transfer of any alcoholic or intoxicating beverage or substance
716	Unauthorized use of over the counter medication or failure to take prescribed medication as required when administered under supervision
736	Possession, manufacture, or introduction of unauthorized keys
750	Indecent exposure
752	Receiving a positive test for use of unauthorized drugs, alcohol, or other intoxicants
830	Any escape from Work Release with voluntary return within 24 hours

Category B-10 classification points
LEVEL 3

Infraction

503	Extortion, blackmail, demanding or receiving money or anything of value in return for protection against others, or under threat of informing
506	Threatening another with bodily harm or with any offense against another person, property, or family
509	Refusing a direct order by any staff member to proceed to or disperse from a particular area
525	Violating conditions of a furlough
558	Interfering with staff members, medical personnel, firefighters, or law enforcement personnel in the performance of their duties
600	Tampering with, damaging, blocking or interfering with any locking or security device
605	Impersonating any staff member, contracted staff member, volunteer, other offender, or visitor
653	Causing an inaccurate count or interfering with count by means of unauthorized absence, hiding, concealing oneself, or other form of deception or distraction

654	Counterfeiting, forgery, altering, falsification, or unauthorized reproduction of any document, article of identification, money, security, or official paper
660	Unauthorized possession of money or other negotiable instruments the value of which is five dollars or more
709	Out-of-bounds: Being in another offenders cell or being in an area in the facility with one or more offenders without authorization
738	Possession of clothing of a staff member
739	Possession of personal information about currently employed staff, contractors, or volunteers, or their immediate family members, not voluntarily given to the offender by the individual involved; including but not limited to: Social security numbers, unpublished home addresses or telephone numbers, driver license numbers, medical, personnel, financial, or real estate records, bank or credit card numbers, or other like information not authorized by the courts or superintendent
745	Refusing to transfer to another institution
746	Engaging in or inciting an organized hunger strike
762	Failing to complete or administrative termination from DOSA substance abuse treatment program. **This infraction must initiated by authorized staff and heard by a Community Corrections Hearing Officer in accordance with WAC 137-24
777	Causing injury to another person by resisting orders, resisting assisted movement or physical efforts to restrain
813	Unauthorized/unaccounted time in the community or being in an unauthorized location in the community
814	While in work release, violation of an imposed special condition
831	While in work release, failure to return from an authorized sign out
879	Operating a motor vehicle without permission or in an unauthorized manner or location

Category C-5 classification points
LEVEL 1

Infraction

| 508 | Throwing objects, materials, substances or spitting in the direction of another person(s) |

517	Committing any act that is a misdemeanor and that is not otherwise included in these rules
555	Theft of property or possession of stolen property
557	Refusing to participate in education or work program or other mandatory programming assignment
563	Making false fire alarm or tampering with, damaging, blocking, or interfering with fire alarms, fire extinguishers, fire hoses, fire exits, or other fire fighting equipment or devices
610	Unauthorized possession of prescribed medication greater than a single or daily dose
620	Receipt or possession of contraband during participation in off-grounds or outer perimeter activity or work detail
659	Sexual harassment
663	Using physical force, intimidation, or coercion against any person
702	Possession, manufacture, or introduction of an unauthorized tool
708	Organizing or participating in unauthorized group activity or meeting
714	Giving, selling, borrowing, lending, or trading money or anything of value to, or accepting or purchasing money or anything of value from, another offender or that offender's friend(s) or family, the value of which is ten dollars or more
717	Causing a threat of injury to another person by resisting orders, resisting assisted movement, or physical efforts to restrain
720	Flooding a cell or another area of the institution/facility
724	Refusing a cell or housing assignment
734	Participating or engaging in the activities of any unauthorized club, organization, gang, or security threat group; or wearing or possessing the symbols of an unauthorized club, organization, gang, or security threat group
810	Failure to seek/maintain employment or training or maintaining oneself financially or being terminated from a job for negative or standard performance

CateGORY C-5 CLASSIFICATION POINTS
LEVEL 2

INFRACTION

552	Causing an innocent person to be penalized or proceeded against by providing false information
554	Damaging or destroying state property or any other item, the value of which is ten dollars or more and that is not in the personal property of the offender
559	Gambling; possession of gambling paraphernalia
656	Giving, receiving, or offering any person a bribe or anything of value for an unauthorized favor or service
706	Giving false information when proposing a release plan
710	Being tattooed while incarcerated, tattooing another, or possessing tattoo paraphernalia
718	Use of mail or telephone in violation with court order or local, state, or federal law
726	Telephoning or sending written communication or otherwise initiating communication with a minor without the approval of that minor's parent or guardian
727	Telephoning or sending written communications to any person contrary to previous written warnings and/or documented disciplinary action
728	Possession of any sexually explicit material(s), as defined by Department policy and/or WAC 137-25-020
740	Fraud, embezzlement or obtaining goods, services, money, or anything of value under false pretense
742	A pattern of creating a false emergency by feigning illness
778	Providing a urine specimen that has been diluted, substituted or altered in any way

Category C-5 classification points
LEVEL 3

Infraction

551	Providing false information to the disciplinary hearing officer or on a disciplinary appeal
606	Possession, introduction, or transfer of any tobacco, tobacco products, matches, or tobacco paraphernalia
657	Being found guilty of four or more general infractions, arising out of separate incidents, within a 90 day period
658	Failing to comply with any administrative or post-hearing sanction imposed for committing a general or serious infraction
662	Soliciting goods or services for which the provider would expect payment when the offender knows or should know that no funds are available to pay for those goods or services
712	Attempted suicide as determined by mental health staff
713	Self-mutilation or self-harm
741	Theft of food the value of which is more than five dollars
755	Misuse or waste of issued supplies, goods, services, or property the replacement value of which is ten dollars or more
811	Entering into an unauthorized contract
812	Failure to report/turn in all earnings income
861	Performing or taking part in an unauthorized marriage

Glossary

Administrative segregation (Ad-Seg)
An offender may be assigned to Ad-Seg when he

  a. Poses a threat to life, property, self, staff, other offenders, or the orderly running of the facility

  b. Requests protection or is deemed by staff to require protection

  c. Is pending a transfer to a more secure facility

All offenders on Ad-Seg are placed in segregation pending an investigation. The investigation cannot last longer than eighty-four days, when the prisoner is either released to population or placed in the Intensive Management Unit.

Band room
A room on the prison grounds where offenders can go to play musical instruments and/or record their own music.

Bitch
See punk.

Bones
Slang term for playing dominoes.

Camp
When a prisoner has less than four years to serve, he becomes eligible for a low security camp. The camp has community and forest work available.

Cell confinement
A period during which offenders are confined to their cells for disciplinary purposes. They are allowed out only for meals, work, school, or visits. Offenders are allowed to take a ten-minute shower and make a phone call every day.

Cell search
An offender's cell is searched by two officers once a month or at any time if there is any suspicion of contraband.

Chain bag (duck bag)
A bag given to each newly arriving offender containing essential items such as soap, toothbrush, toothpaste, and institution information.

Chain boxes
Two boxes of personal property that the offender may bring with him on the chain bus while being transferred at the state's cost. Any items not fitting in these two boxes must be sent at the offender's expense by mail.

Chain day
The one day out of the week when offenders are transferred into and out of a prison.

Chain of command
All prisons run through two chains of commands. The administrative chain of command from the highest to lowest level is as follows: superintendent, associate superintendent, custody program manager (CPM), custody unit supervisor (CUS), and counselor. The daily in-prison command is as follows: captain, lieutenant, CPM, CUS, sergeant, and guards.

Chapel
The area inside the prison designated for offenders to engage in religious studies, programs, and worship.

Charge
The crime that an offender is convicted of.

Chow hall
The area where the prisoners have their meals.

Clallam Bay Corrections Center (CBCC)
Located in Forks, Washington, Clallam Bay is a closed and medium custody facility that houses around eight hundred prisoners. It has two segregation units, a short-term segregation unit, an Intensive Management Unit for long-term segregation, four closed custody units, and four medium custody units.

Classification and facility plan review
Classification is a management tool used to assign offenders to the least restrictive custody designation while meeting the need to provide for the safety of the public, staff, and other offenders. The classification system is designed to encourage offender participation in work, education, treatment, and vocational programming in a manner that results in movement to a less restrictive custody level.

Cliques
Term used to describe different groups or associations.

Clothing room
Area of the prison where offender go to either be issued state clothing, exchange damaged clothing items for new ones, or return state clothing prior to release or transfer.

Closed custody
The highest level of security for prisoners, which is established by an offender's custody points. Closed custody is for offenders with seriously violent crimes, who exhibit consistently violent behavior in prison, or who just cannot abide by the prison regulations. Closed custody points are 0 to 39.

CO
A correctional officer.

Counselor
A staff member who is a part of the custody staff. The counselor oversees a caseload of offenders assigned to him or her by the CUS. The counselor is responsible for but not limited to offenders' concerns, classification reviews/plans and assisting offenders in release planning, education enrollment, and job assignment.

Cuff port
Small key-operated opening on the cell doors generally used for purposes such as applying handcuffs to the wrist and inserting a meal tray.

Custody unit supervisor (CUS)
A staff member who presides over the offenders and staff of his or her designated living unit. The CUS is responsible for classification reviews, offender representatives/liaisons, special offender concerns, and the safe and orderly operation of the unit. The CUS is fourth in the chain of command (see "chain of command").

Custody staff
There are four levels an officer can attain: officer, sergeant, lieutenant, and captain. They are in charge of the safety and security of the facility.

Dayroom
Common area in the unit where offenders can congregate to do things such as converse, play cards and board games, shower, and make phone calls.

DCC
Days of cell confinement.

DDS (D-Seg)
Days of disciplinary segregation.

Deductions
Any money an offender receives in the mail is subject to a deduction, from 35 to 95 percent. The lowest is 35 percent, which includes 10 percent that to the offender's mandatory savings account (which the offender will receive upon release), 20 percent for the cost of incarceration, and 5 percent for a crime victim compensation fund. Up to 95 percent can be taken for various reasons, such as child support, legal and financial obligations, and institutional debts.

DGTCL
Days of good time credit lost for committing an infraction or not programming.

Disciplinary segregation
Term describing when an offender is placed in the hole while waiting for an infraction hearing or is sentenced at a hearing to the hole for a set number of days.

Dope
Hard drugs, which offenders usually snort or inject.

Drug/alcohol testing
Targeted and random substance abuse testing that the department performs.

Dry cell search
After reasonable suspicion has been established, an offender is placed in a secure room/cell during the safe recovery of internally concealed foreign substances, instruments, or other contraband.

Ducks
Commonly used name given to all newly arriving offenders at an institution.

ERD
Earliest release date from prison.

Fella
One of "the guys." An offender who is in good standing among his peers.

Fish
See duck.

Fishing
Devising a makeshift rope for the purpose of sliding it under your door crack and passing stuff from cell to cell.

Flag
Typically, a folded piece of paper hung in a cell door or out the bars to let the other offenders know you don't want to be disturbed.

Grievance coordinator
Grievances can be filed by any offender for any situation that cannot be resolved by the first four officers in the chain of command. When the grievance is filed, the grievance coordinator hears the complaint and investigates the concern. Taking into account the policy and the issue at hand, the grievance coordinator will give an unbiased resolution to the complaint.

Guard tower
A tall concrete structure in or around the prison used as a vantage point by correctional officers to oversee day-to-day activities.

Hearings
Formal meeting between an offender and hearings officer or prison administrators.

Hepatitis C
A non-curable blood disease that is passed easily by direct blood-to-blood contact.

HIV
A non-curable blood disease passed through contact with infected blood. HIV is an early form of AIDS. It is passed by fighting, tattooing, sharing needles, and having unprotected sex.

Hobby shop
An area of the prison where offenders can work on their arts and crafts projects.

Hole
The place where prisoners are segregated for disciplinary, administrative, or protective custody purposes.

Homie
A term used to describe a friend or associate.

Hustler
One who uses his skills to acquire whatever he needs.

Identification cards (IDs)
All individuals—staff, volunteers, and offenders—are issued ID cards, which they must display on their upper-left breast at all times.

Internal investigation department (I & I)
Detectives that investigate any staff, visitors, correctional officers, or offenders that they feel need to be investigated.

Intensive management unit (IMU)
An offender deemed to present an immediate and serious threat to the safety and security of the institution, staff, self, and/or other offenders by

- a. A serious infraction

- b. Consistent behavioral/infraction problems

- c. Acts that present a risk

All IMU offenders live in segregation but are on a level system where they can earn privileges such as magazines, newspapers, store, TV, and radios.

Kite
A form that offenders send for requests and questions to any department within the prison.

Law library
An area containing a variety of legal materials and law books, which offenders can use for legal research.

Library
An area inside the prison where books, magazines, newspapers, and other reading and viewing materials are kept and may be checked out by the offender.

Lifer
An offender sentenced to spend the rest of his life in prison.

Lockdowns
When a situation arises that threatens the safe and secure operation of the institution, all offenders will be locked in their cell until the situation is investigated and the prison is cleared for normal operations.

Long-term offender
An offender that is serving a sentence of more than ten years.

Mainline
A term used to describe living within the main population.

Mainlining
When someone injects drugs into their veins using a needle.

Major infraction (serious infraction)
An infraction that is more severe that a general infraction and carries a more harsh sanction. All major infractions can carry segregation time and loss of classification points for a predetermined period.

Mcneil Island Corrections Center (MICC)
Located across the water from Steilacoom, Washington, the island has five units with a mix of long-term and short-term minimum custody prisoners. It has a segregation unit for short-term segregation and an Intensive Management Unit

(IMU) for long-term segregation offenders. The prison houses about eight hundred prisoners.

Medical floor
The medical floor contains mental health, dental, and doctors' offices.

Medical hold
A hold placed on an offender by the medical department for a variety of medical reasons. This can place limitations on such things as custody, transfers, recreation use, and jobs an offender can have.

Medium custody
A custody level established by an offender's custody points, from 40 to 54. Medium custody is for long-term offenders with serious violent crimes and offenders that are less violent but cause minor problems.

Medium security unit
Located next to the penitentiary in Walla Walla, Washington. The Medium Security Unit houses about eight hundred medium custody prisoners in four units.

Minimum custody
A custody level established by an offender's custody points, from 55 to 67. Minimum custody is for offenders who require less supervision and are more prepared for their release.

Minor infraction (general infraction)
An infraction that is less severe than a major infraction and carries a less harsh punishment. Minor infractions do not carry segregation time or loss of classification points.

Mission boy
An offender whom other offenders use to do their dirty work.

Mule
Anyone who smuggles contraband into a facility.

Needle
Used in a prison setting to inject drugs. Also known as points, rigs, and binkys.

Orientation
All offenders arriving at or transferred to a new institution are provided specific information about that facility at an orientation class.

Pat search
A superficial search of an offender, conducted by a correctional officer. In this search, the officer's hands pass over the body on the outside of the clothing to ensure the absence of concealed contraband.

Paperwork
A collection of forms and other papers given to all convicted. Includes information such as the offender's crimes and past crimes.

Personal laundry room
A room in the units, wing, or pods that has washers and dryers you can use for personal clothes.

Personal property
Non-state-issued property either sent to an offender by family and friends or purchased by the offender from an outside vendor or the institutional store.

Phones
All phones in every institution are by collect call only. When an offender dials a number, he is asked to enter an eight-digit offender personal identification number (OPIN). This number allows the state to record all phone numbers the offender calls and possibly monitor the phone calls. Calls cannot last more than twenty minutes and cost upwards of $3.50 each.

Pods
A part of the units where the offenders live.

Points
A tool used by the Department of Corrections to classify where and what type of facility an offender is placed in. Every offender is given a set number of points based on his or her crime, age, sentence, prior convictions, institutional conduct, and other criteria.

Policy
A written set of rules or procedures the Department of Corrections makes and follows.

Prison daddy
Term used for a stronger offender who is typically in control of a "punk" or a "bitch."

Prison gay
An offender who never engages in homosexual activities outside a prison setting but has consensual sex with men while incarcerated.

Prison rules
Rules that exist within the prison by other offenders. These rules are unwritten but well known and followed.

Procedures
The written steps that the Department of Corrections makes and follows that all employees and offenders use to guide their actions in prison.

Property room
The area of the prison where offenders go to pick up new personal property items, pick up personal property shipped from other institutions, and mail out property items.

Protective custody (PC)
Where an offender is removed from the prison population for his or her own protection by his or her own request or request of the administration. This is usually accompanied by a subsequent transfer or long term segregation.

Punk
An offender, usually a weaker individual and/or a sex offender, who is used for the sole purpose of satisfying another offender's gratifications.

Receiving units
Located within the Washington State Corrections Center in Shelton, Washington, the receiving units are used to classify new prisoners and as a transferring base for prisoners being transferred from one facility to another. There are five units that house about one thousand prisoners.

Rotunda
Area outside the pods or wings, which usually includes the guards'/sergeant's office and an entrance to the unit's control booth.

Segregation
Offenders are housed in segregation for disciplinary, administrative, or protective custody purposes. In the segregation units, the offenders are housed in a bare cell for at least twenty-three hours a day. They are allowed out only for showers and no more than one hour of recreation.

Sentence
The punishment allotted to each offender, including the amount of time an offender must serve, the amount of money an offender must pay in fines, the amount of time an offender must spend on community supervision, and any other stipulations set forth by the courts.

Seperatee
When a prisoner fears another prisoner for any reason, he can ask to have a "keep separate" placed between them. If granted, the two prisoners can never be in the same prison at the same time. The administration or courts can also place keep separates for any reason, but they are used mostly for co-defendants or when prisoners cause too many problems together.

Sergeant
A staff member who has advanced one rank beyond the lowest grade of correctional officer. The sergeant is responsible for offenders' concerns, cell regulations/moves, offender representatives/liaisons, and the safe and orderly operation of their post. He is fifth in the chain of command (see Chain of Command),

Sex beef
Slang term used to describe any sex crime.

Shank
A prison-made knife.

Shoe program
See Intensive Management Unit (IMU).

Short-term offender
An offender that is serving a sentence of ten years or less.

Snitch
A slang term used to describe an informant inside the prison.

State gear
See state issued clothing.

State-issued clothing
The Department of Corrections provides state-issued clothing to all offenders upon reception at a facility. Clothing usually includes pants, underwear, T-shirts, work shirts, coat, belt, sock, and shoes.

State laundry
A department that hires offenders to wash all the offenders' state clothing and bedding, using industrial washers and dryers.

Store
Term used for the prison commissary, where offenders may purchase items such as food, drinks, toiletries, and personal property. A store purchase request may be placed by an offender weekly, and it is delivered to his unit (except for property items, which must be placed on his personal property matrix and issued through the property room).

Strip search
An offender is stripped of all his clothing and instructed to expose all areas of his body so they may be searched for contraband.

Superintendent
Every institution has a superintendent. The superintendent oversees the overall operation of his institution, including the offenders, officers, all other staff members, and volunteers. The superintendent grants final approval on all paperwork, including classification, reviews, and policy changes.

Support staff
There are five levels of support staff: counselor, custody unit supervisor (CUS), custody program manager (CPM), associate superintendents, and superintendent. They are in charge of administration and custody issues.

Tattoo
Very common in prison. Inmates are frequently tattooed in showers, dayrooms, gyms, yards, doorways, and anywhere else they can go without being seen by the guards. All tattooing is done by cell-made tattoo guns and supplies. Tattoo ink is usually obtained from pens or made from different prison-sanctioned ingredients, but it is sometimes smuggled into the prison.

Tattoo guns
Tattoo guns are made from motors found in radios, electric razors, and fans.

Tier check
Routine walk-through of the living unit conducted by a correctional officer, usually accompanied by a brief glance into each individual cell to make sure things are running in an orderly fashion.

Trailer visits (extended family visits)
Term for a visit between an offender and his family that takes place inside a manufactured home on the prison grounds for a predetermined length of time. Only immediate family is eligible.

Transfer
A formal, orchestrated move of an offender from one institution to another.

Twin rivers corrections center (trcc)
Located in Monroe, Washington, Twin Rivers has two minimum-custody units and two medium-custody units, mostly for short-term prisoners. One medium unit is used to house offenders in the Sex Offender Treatment Program. Twin Rivers houses about eight hundred prisoners.

Unit
A unit is where the offenders' cells are located. All units have wings, pods, or tiers within them.

Urine testing (UAS)
An offender is strip-searched by two officers and observed urinating in a cup. These may be ordered randomly or if the offender is under suspicion of illegal substance abuse.

Visiting application
A form that needs to be filled out and returned to the institution before any friends or family can visit. Once the form is approved, the visitor is allowed to visit the offender at any institution he is placed in.

Visiting list
An official list of people in the outside world who have sent in a form and been approved to visit with an offender. All visitors must be approved before being allowed entrance.

Visit room
An area in the prison designated for visitation between offenders and their family and/or friends.

Washington State Corrections Center (WSCC)
Located in Shelton, Washington, the Correction Center has three units for short- and long-term medium and minimum custody offenders. There are also five units used for receiving of transferring prisoners and classification of new prisoners. There are about one thousand six hundred prisoners housed in this facility.

Washington State Reformatory (WSR)
Located in Monroe, Washington, the reformatory has four closed custody units that have about one hundred bunks for long-term medium custody offenders and a segregation unit for short-term segregation. It houses about eight hundred mostly long-term offenders. There is an Intensive Management Unit outside the prison walls that houses about three hundred long-term segregation prisoners.

Washington State Penitentiary (WSP)
Located in Walla Walla, Washington, the penitentiary has about fifteen hundred prisoners housed in three closed custody wings, one protective custody unit, and two segregation units. There is an Intensive Management Unit (IMU) built outside the walls for three hundred long-term segregation prisoners.

Weight pile
Area where weights are used.

Welching
Agreeing to do something and then not doing it.

Wing
A part of the unit where the offenders live. Walla Walla calls its main living units wings. These are large living units.

Wood
Slang term used to describe a white guy in good standing.

Index

www.ingramcontent.com/pod-product-compliance
Lightning Source LLC
Chambersburg PA
CBHW022232290526
45785CB00014B/746